DINOSAUR IN PERMAFROST

by

BILL KINCAID

With cartoons by

Jim Potts

Bruno,

Happy Christmas,

Bill

Published by

TheSAURAS Ltd

Published by:

TheSAURAS Ltd

10 Crutchfield Lane, Walton-on-Thames, Surrey KT12 2QZ

Tel: 01932 227827. Fax: 01932 269445
e-mail: billkincaid@tinyworld.co.uk
Editor: Rebecca Kincaid

ISBN 0-9540444-1-X

Produced in Great Britain by:
Alden Press Ltd
Osney Mead, Oxford OX2 0EF

ABOUT THE AUTHOR

Bill Kincaid served for 36 years in the Army, half of which period was spent in the Ministry of Defence in a succession of posts dealing with the procurement of defence equipment. His last job was as Director of Operational Requirements for all land systems equipment.

Since 1995, he has worked as a consultant to the Ministry of Defence and to the defence industry, where he has gained further experience of the changing defence procurement world. He has lectured on equipment procurement to the Royal Institute of International Affairs, The Royal United Services Institute for Defence Studies, the Royal Military College of Science, the UK Defence Forum, The Joint Services Command and Staff College, RAF Cranwell and to various defence companies and commercial conferences in this country and in the USA.

His sell-out book of 1997, *A Dinosaur in Whitehall*, was a hard-hitting, controversial criticism of what was wrong with defence equipment procurement at that time. Many of his recommendations for improvement subsequently found their way into the Government's Smart Procurement Initiative. His follow-up to this, *Dancing with the Dinosaur*, examining the way in which the early implementation of the Smart Procurement Initiative was being carried out, is on its third reprint and is required reading at the Royal Military College of Science and the Joint Services Command and Staff College.

Tel: 01932 227827
Fax: 01932 269445
billkincaid@tinyworld.co.uk.

PREFACE

"Smart Procurement is running out of steam."

Such is the common perception today amongst those involved in the business of defence equipment acquisition, whether they are from the Ministry of Defence or the defence industry. While acknowledging the efforts that MOD has made so far (although not conceding improvement in output), these individuals believe that Ministers and senior MOD officials have placed a 'tick-in-the-box' against Smart Procurement and are now giving higher priority to other defence issues. Do Ministers believe we are on track to revolutionise defence procurement, as was the original vision?

"A revolution... a complete cultural change in Ministry of Defence procurement."[1]

If they do, it is because top MOD officials have told them that we are; not surprisingly, as they have set their own targets and are now declaring that they have met them or are at least on track to meet them. They have a vested interest in declaring 'success'. There is certainly progress, some of it important. But revolution? An unquantified improvement seems to be the limit of ambition today, not the revolutionary approach suggested by the unofficial MOD/industry slogan in the Winter of 1997/8:

"On time in half the time at 30% less cost."

That's revolution. That's what we need. But are we going to get it? Probably not, because it seems too difficult. Yet, it is possible to revolutionise defence procurement, but it needs clear vision, a strong

---

[1] *UK Defence Review: A Cut Above the Rest*, Sir Robert Walmsley, Chief of Defence Procurement, Interavia, September 1998.

collective will and determined political leadership, none of which is much in evidence right now.

My earlier book, *Dancing with the Dinosaur*, looked at the way Smart Procurement was being implemented in the early days, some two-and-a-half years ago. Then progress was necessarily limited, but there was much hope. Today, there is clearly greater progress, but what are expectations now?

This book attempts to chart that progress and identify areas of stagnation and regression. It also tries to answer two questions: Will Smart Procurement work? And, if not, what can we do if we are serious about revolutionising defence equipment procurement?

This book refers repeatedly to the earlier *Dancing with the Dinosaur* particularly for detail about the theory of Smart Procurement and the difficulties in implementing some of it. Those who know the subject will not need to turn up the references, but those who are not, or who want to delve deeper, may find the earlier book complementary.

A word on the dreaded subject of acronyms, which plague most walks of life, but perhaps none more so than defence. I have spelt out each in full the first time it appears. Those that keep recurring, I have not spelt out again, whereas those that recur occasionally have been spelt out each time they appear after a gap as a painless reminder. This may appear inconsistent, but it is done with the idea of helping those readers with less background who may find the acronyms a pain. If this fails, there is a Glossary at Appendix Two.

I am indebted to all those who gave of their time to discuss their views with me. They spoke off the record, so I cannot attribute quotes or particular views, but this allowed them to speak their minds without constraint. The most striking thing about their views is that they are almost entirely consistent; differences in emphasis, perhaps, but not in essence. This makes me confident that the position described in the following pages is as accurate as it can be.

Officialdom would be well advised to take heed. I wonder if it will.

Bill Kincaid
July 2002

CONTENTS

INTRODUCTION:

TACKLING THE PROBLEM

CHAPTER ONE

TACKLING THE PROBLEM

By 1995, it was widely recognised that Ministry of Defence procurement of defence equipment was in a mess. Project costs escalated wildly, project schedules slipped significantly, more than 80% of in-service dates (ISD) were missed and many key performance parameters were not met. Above all, the average project was taking some two decades in the procurement process before it was fielded.

This was nothing new.[2] However, during the early 1980s, this was masked by the annual 3% increase in defence funding in real terms but, when defence spending flattened and then began a steep decline as the 'Peace Dividend' was extracted from 1989 onwards, the problems became starker. Politicians and senior Ministry officials were unwilling to grasp the nettle, and the Defence Costs Study, or 'Front Line First', hardly touched procurement organisation, process or culture. Heads were stuck firmly in the sand. After 17 years in power, the Tories were hardly going to admit to the existence of a long-running sore.

The situation in 1997, when Labour was elected, is described in detail in my book *A Dinosaur in Whitehall*,[3] and the key problems then included:

- A lack of personal accountability, with responsibility and authority badly matched.

- A lack of professionalism.

---

[2] For a historical perspective see *Dancing with the Dinosaur*, Bill Kincaid, UK Defence Forum, December 1999

[3] *A Dinosaur in Whitehall*, Bill Kincaid, Brassey's, September 1997

- A consensus-committee culture, leading to weak decision-making.

- Convoluted procedures.

- Stifling but ineffective scrutiny.

The new Labour government immediately announced the Strategic
Defence Review which was to include:

"*A ruthless examination of how value for money for defence procurement, one of the most important aspects of the review, can be improved... we are looking for 'smart procurement'.*"[4]

> *A ruthless examination of value for money*

Smart Procurement had been born.

The Main Problems

In November 1997, the new government called in the consultants
McKinsey, who found the major problems to be:

- Early stages of the procurement cycle were ineffective, unproductive and under-resourced.

- The process was too reliant on technical specifications.

- There was too much reliance on competitive tendering.

- Project management was weak.

- There was too little delegation.

- Key people spent too short a period in post.

- There was low accountability.

- There was poor scrutiny.

- Carrots and sticks were too small.

---

[4] House of Commons Defence Committee, Eighth Report 1997/8, *SDR*, Volume 1, Paragraph 333

These findings bore a striking resemblance to those discussed in my book, *A Dinosaur in Whitehall*, which had been published a couple of months before, but should have come as no surprise as the problems were clearly understood at least at the working and middle management levels. It was, in effect, common ground.

Further work identified more problems, chief of which were that, within MOD, there was no clear, single customer for equipment projects and that a number of processes were managed separately, making an effective whole life approach impossible.

The Recommended Initiatives

Diagnosing the problems was one thing; identifying adequate solutions was more difficult. However, by July 1998 the Ministry announced the following initiatives:

Identifying adequate solutions was more difficult

- Creation of a clear MOD internal Customer/Supplier relationship by reorganising the Operational Requirements staff, the Procurement Executive and the single-Service logistics organisations.

- Streamlined procedures including changes to the Downey Cycle.

- Incremental Acquisition to allow fielding of equipment of a less ambitious capability which would then be upgraded in several lower-risk stages.

- A Through-Life Concept to ensure that decisions would be taken on a broader view of the equipment's life cycle and making trade-offs between military requirements, costs and timescales.

- Partnering to involve industry more closely in the development of operational requirements and equipment designs.

- Personal accountability to improve time and cost estimating.

- Integrated Project Teams (IPTs), consisting of all stakeholders and scientific staff as well as industry when competition allows, with a clear leader having authority to make trade-off decisions and who would retain responsibility for equipment after it had entered service.

A Smart Procurement Implementation Team (SPIT — an unfortunate acronym which was later changed to SPRINT) was formed in September 1998 and was driven hard by the then Secretary of State for Defence, George Robertson, and particularly by the then Under-Secretary of State, John Spellar, who had been given ministerial responsibility for Smart Procurement. The importance of this strong political leadership by these two Ministers should not be underestimated because, without it, Smart Procurement would have been strangled at birth by senior figures in MOD who were uneasy about the changes that were required.

> *The importance of this strong political leadership should not be underestimated*

Dancing with the Dinosaur

Early implementation focused on reorganisation and process change but, while these made a valuable base on which to build, in themselves could not deliver the revolutionary progress that was so badly needed.

In December 1999 I published *Dancing with the Dinosaur*, which looked at how Smart Procurement was being implemented and what issues were and were not being tackled. The conclusions were spread over three chapters — one each for MOD, industry and MOD partnering industry. Progress, where it had been made, was clearly identified and weaknesses in implementation, which not surprisingly at that point were more numerous, were spelled out. Where the theory appeared to be flawed, issues for further thought were explored. The position at that point can be read in the final three chapters of the book.[5]

---

[5] *Dancing with the Dinosaur*, Bill Kincaid, UK Defence Forum, December 1999, pp 343–362

Briefly, implementation by December 1999 could be summed up as follows:

- Real progress at that date was very limited and reversible.
- There were many weaknesses in how Smart Procurement was being implemented which would undermine the possibility of significant benefits in the future.
- There were numerous issues that needed further thought and/or resolution.
- Industry had not 'bought in' to Smart Procurement.

The Smart Procurement Initiative had correctly identified the objective, but the path that was being mapped out would only reach that objective if the existing weaknesses and immaturities were to be resolved satisfactorily.

An Intelligent Dinosaur?

In the two-and-a-half years since the publication of *Dancing with the Dinosaur*, much defence water has flowed under the Whitehall bridge. Smart Procurement has been rebranded as Smart Acquisition, Ministers have changed and September 11th 'changed the world'. Other imperatives have overtaken procurement improvement as flavours of the year, but the need to get better value for every procurement pound remains just as important as it was in 1997, and it is necessary to examine the position once again to answer some key questions. For example, has progress in those 30 months been as great as hoped for, or has it trailed away? Are politicians and senior officials maintaining the pressure or have they placed a fat tick in the box and moved on to new imperatives? Are we on the way to achieving immense savings in procurement or are we allowing the Dinosaur to return to old habits and squander

Are we allowing the Dinosaur to return to old habits?

billions of pounds per year? Above all, do top officials have a clear view of Smart Procurement implementation today?

In the Winter and Spring of 2001/2, I embarked on a major exercise to seek the views of over one hundred people in MOD and industry, at all management levels, to get a wide view of what the perceived position was. My findings were hardly unexpected, but what was surprising was that the views were almost entirely consistent. I think we can accept those views as accurate, even though they vary considerably from the 'spin' put out from official sources.

PART ONE:

PROGRESS, STAGNATION AND REGRESSION

CHAPTER TWO

ORGANISATIONAL CHANGE

A great deal of effort, which generated considerable heat at times, was initially focused on organisational change within the MOD. The key changes set in motion were:

- The creation of a central MOD customer, by merging the Systems and Programmes areas to create Equipment Capability (EC).

- The conversion of the Procurement Executive into an agency – the Defence Procurement Agency (DPA).

- The integration of the three single-Service logistics organisations into the joint Defence Logistics Organisation (DLO).

- The privatisation of the Defence Evaluation and Research Agency (DERA).

PROGRESS

Reorganisation

Those four major changes have now been completed, although the fourth became a part-privatisation with some three-quarters of DERA becoming the privatised QinetiQ, and the remainder being retained within the MOD as the Defence Scientific and Technical Laboratory (Dstl).

The most significant change is the creation of Equipment Capability, not because it considers 'capability' rather than 'operational requirements', but because it can now function as the clear central MOD customer for acquisition of equipment, a role that the former

Operational Requirements (OR) division could not discharge because its Chief had no authority over the Equipment Plan. Now the Deputy Chief of the Defence Staff (Equipment Capability) (DCDS(EC)) — a three-star post — has both responsibility and authority and is therefore accountable: he is 'empowered'. This is one of the most significant advances so far.

> *The creation of 'Equipment Capability' as the clear central MOD customer*

Empowerment

Empowerment has been a feature at lower levels, too. Within the DPA and DLO, Integrated Project Teams (IPTs) have been formed under an empowered team leader, who is now able to make many more decisions, without referral upwards, than previously. Of course, the best project managers of the past made as many decisions but many of these had to be done clandestinely. As the late Peter Merritt, an outstanding project manager, said:

> *"The first rule in the MOD is to find out what rules you cannot break, then bend them as far as possible."*

Now, decisions by IPT leaders are officially OK. An advance without doubt.

In EC, Directors of Equipment Capability (DECs — mostly one-star officers) have been empowered. It is they who decide, within their own area, the priority of each capability or project, and, when savings are needed, which ones have to be moved to the right, reduced in scale or terminated.

EC/DPA Relationships

While at certain levels the relationship between the Central Customer (EC) and its supplier (DPA) is uneasy and, at times, downright

> *The vital ingredient is the success of the Requirements Manager*

difficult, at the key level it is now very close with IPT leaders working harmoniously with the relevant DEC or DECs. Perhaps the vital ingredient is the successful creation of the Requirements Manager — EC's 'man in the IPT' — whose difficult dual responsibility to DEC and IPT could have scuppered things. But it has not, and credit is due to DECs, IPT leaders and, especially, to individual Requirements Managers.

But we should not think that the MOD internal Customer/ Supplier relationship during the procurement stages is wholly successful. There are tensions, and these could well worsen as more projects pass Main Gate and get straitjacketed by tough cost, time and performance parameters. Moreover, the good relationships are not necessarily a product of Smart Procurement, as there were many such relationships in the past when branch colonels in OR, project managers, users and support managers worked closely, harmoniously and effectively together, particularly in areas where there was strong single-Service or capbadge proponency. Where this proponency was less clear (e.g. ISTAR, C4, NBC), relationships were more distant, and it is in these areas that the real progress has occurred.

Now, the problems generated are caused more by a mismatch between EC's capability organisation and DPA's project organisation, which creates the need for one IPT leader to interface with more than one DEC on a particular project, or a DEC to work with many IPT leaders within different Peer Groups on a single programme. This mismatch in organisation gives rise to a clear lack of unity of both purpose and common goals,

> *A clear lack of unity of purpose*

although perhaps this is not new. The DPA organisation merits a re-look, so that each peer group, for example, is aligned with a particular DEC.

STAGNATION

The Through-Life IPT

The Smart Procurement Initiative gave priority to creating a clear Customer/Supplier relationship within MOD,[6] with the Central Customer (EC) dictating its capability requirements to its Supplier (the DPA) during procurement, and the Service Customer (the Commanders-in-Chief) being supported during the in-service life of the equipment by its supplier (the DLO). Responsibility was to be handed over from the DPA to the DLO at the ISD, with the IPT transferring from the DPA to the DLO at that point. This was always a naive view of life, for things are far more complex than that.[7] For one thing, more than 90% of projects lie within 'cluster' or multi-project IPTs which cannot be transferred from DPA to DLO when one of its projects reaches ISD because the remainder will be at various other stages in the procurement cycle. For another, even single-project IPTs seem unable to transfer with its individual members, because those members do not wish to move their place of work from Bristol to Andover or Whitton.

The result is that all projects are effectively 'thrown over the wall' to the DLO at a critical juncture. This inevitably causes major disruption. If the IPT leader is responsible for the pro-

> *The result is that projects are 'thrown over the wall' to the DLO*

ject only until ISD, how much effort will he put into support arrangements for the future? And if funding is split between the DPA IPT (for procurement) and the DLO IPT (for support), when each IPT has many other projects, how transparent is that funding allocation and use and how can changes to the balance of funding be effected? Furthermore, if the contract is placed with a company for production

---

[6] *Dancing with the Dinosaur*, Bill Kincaid, UK Defence Forum, December 1999, Chapter 3

[7] Ibid, page 58

and initial support (say, for ten years), how good will the support part of the contract be if written by the DPA IPT contract officer who may have little or no experience of either working in the DLO or of DLO support contracts?

Throwing projects over the wall destroys continuity, corporate knowledge and accountability. A complete change of personnel is not what is required at ISD. What are needed as the project goes through the various stages of procurement and support are:

- Graduated changes in IPT role.

- Related changes in IPT objectives.

- Controlled changes of personnel and expertise.

It is perhaps not surprising that the separation between DPA and DLO gives rise to:

- Serious difficulties with the Through-Life Concept.

- Major complications with allocation, and subsequent modification, of funding for procurement and support.

- Severe criticism by DLO IPTs of many of the support contracts they inherit from DPA IPTs.

Many people see that the only realistic solution is a merger between DPA and DLO, or at least that part of DLO which handles equipment support.

> *The only realistic solution is a merger between DPA and part of DLO*

The Service Customer and Support Costs

Another Customer/Supplier relationship that is not functioning as envisaged is that between the Service Customer and each of the other major elements — EC, DPA and DLO. This is hardly surprising as the staff of the Commanders-in-Chief do not have the numbers or the expertise to discharge their customer role effectively. So, they delegate. Responsibility for, say, a land C2 system might be delegated to the army's Signal Officer-in-Chief, but his staff may also advise the Central Customer, so the taut relationship becomes more complex.

One thing the Service Customer should do early in the procurement cycle is to ensure that running costs are minimised, as 80% are locked in by equipment design before Main Gate. This does not happen, and it is left to EC and DPA to do this... or not. After all, if EC are having difficulties in fitting everything into a financially squeezed Equipment Plan, and if the DPA IPT leader has tough performance, cost and time targets to meet, neither are likely to welcome a cost increase in the near term to achieve possible financial gains in 10 or 15 years' time.

Suppliers Rule OK!

So are the Customers in charge? Hardly. You have only to look at the membership of the Equipment Approvals Committee (EAC) which includes both the Chief of Defence Procurement (CDP) and the Chief of Defence Logistics (CDL) (the two Suppliers) — but not DCDS(EC) or the Commanders-in-Chief (the Central and Service Customers respectively). True, the Vice Chief of the Defence Staff (VCDS) is a member and he is nominally the Customer representative, but he has such a wide remit that he can hardly be expected to drive CDP and CDL. This situation is repeated on the Service Boards. On the Army Board, the 'equipment man' is an XD, a DPA two-star executive director with no direct authority over land programmes, rather than the relevant Capability Manager (CM) from EC.

Until top committee membership includes MOD Customers, rather than Suppliers, the envisaged Customer/Supplier relationship will continue to stutter.

There is, however, one change on the horizon which may well shift the balance between the Central Customer (EC) and its

Supplier (DPA). In the near future, EC will take over the IPT operating costs and so will be able to control the size and life of each IPT.

REGRESSION

Management Posts

Empowerment means that the old management chain is redundant. In effect, IPT leaders in the DPA work direct to the CDP and DECs direct to DCDS(EC). The middle man has been cut out. Or has he? The previous one- and two-star posts are still there in the DPA, now dubbed Executive Directors (XDs) and Support Directors (SDs), and the two-star posts in EC are called CMs. The difference is that they now have little power except as part of the DPA or EC Board which may or may not make important decisions, depending on how their chief executive operates.

In the words of one former IPT leader:

"XDs are trying to find a role, but will it be one which adds value?"

and from another:

> *XDs are trying to find a role, but are they adding value?*

"The Peer Group adds nothing to my IPT."

And from an industrialist who has close association with MOD:

"Peer Groups are not working; they need to be grouped by DECs."

The last comment arises from the original Peer Group idea that groupings by project stages would provide vital cross-fertilisation of ideas within each group. But this was never going to be possible because the majority of IPTs had, and still have, a large number of projects all at different stages of the procurement cycle, so experience gained from one project in, say, the Manufacture Phase only reads across to a few other projects in the whole Peer Group, and this experience is lost by the time that the others reach the same stage some years later.

Peer Groups are important but the groupings need to be re-thought (possibly to reflect DEC organisation). At the same time, the role of their Support Directors needs to be clearly redefined.

Stovepiping

Empowerment, too, leads to another problem: stovepiping. An IPT leader, or DEC, will tend to focus exclusively on his own job requirements. Nothing new here as that is exactly what the former project managers, programme directors and operational requirements directors used to do. But then, the management chain was able to coordinate policy and output across many projects, whereas now that these IPT leaders and DECs are empowered, each can make his own decisions without reference to anybody else. While empowerment has undoubtedly improved efficiency and effectiveness within a single IPT or capability area, it has created a stovepipe effect where each is unconnected with others. The result:

> *Empowerment leads to stovepiping*

- A loss of coherence in procurement output.

- Greater difficulty in driving capability across these stovepipes.

- The Through-Life Concept is made more difficult to implement.

- Commonality of components is seriously threatened.

To be fair, EC is working hard at finding the key to coordinating output across all capability areas, through their Capability Audit, wherein areas of concern are identified, the influences on each tabulated and the resolutions to each are then listed. For example, Suppression of Enemy Air Defences (SEAD) is primarily the responsibility of DEC Theatre Airspace, but there are influences from, and solutions that may exist in whole or part within, DEC Under Water Battlespace, DEC Above Water Battlespace, DEC Indirect Battlefield Engagement and/or DEC ISTAR. These possible influences are then analysed by the Joint Capabilities Board (JCB) members to arrive at capability decisions, although how this last all-important process works is not at all clear, particularly as JCB members are generalists and lack depth of expertise across the board. So, the stovepipes are likely to remain.

While stovepiping may be exacerbated by empowerment, it is not new. However, in the past it has been resolved or at least minimised by the higher management chain. This chain, as has been mentioned, has now been removed from the decision-making process and can no longer act as an integrating body. Nevertheless, the posts at one- and two-star level are still there and should be used to reduce the effects of stovepiping without, however, undermining the advantages that empowerment has brought.

This may sound tricky, and no doubt it is, but is that not what we pay senior staff to do? And is that not what their experience and personal qualities fit them for? We seem to have fallen between two stools by embracing pure empowerment, while retaining senior posts. Would it not be more sensible either to take out these posts (XDs, SDs, CMs) altogether or to retain them and use them more effectively?

There is a wider stovepiping problem. The DPA/DLO divide has already been mentioned, and it is an example of two MOD organisations acting as stovepipes. And there are other such mega-stovepipes. There is, for example, no real audit trail from the work of the Joint Doctrine and Concepts Centre to the Director of Joint Warfare to the DEC, so each operates as a stovepipe, with major implications for such issues as sensors-to-shooters and timelines for engaging fleeting targets. And, as we shall see in Chapter Three, there is a stovepipe effect between the organisation that runs the Equipment Plan (EP) and that which manages the Short Term Plan (STP), the former being managed by EC, the latter by the Principal Finance Officer (PFO).

The MOD is full of stovepipe bodies, and there are further stovepipes within each stovepipe. No wonder people refer to a loss of coherence in procurement output. In the words of one prime contractor executive:

> *No wonder people refer to a loss of coherence in procurement output*

> *"The system of prime contractors taking total responsibility is destroying the commonality which was achieved with such effort over the years. The prime contractor now fits what he decides and the Services get a wider and wider selection of such things as batteries, engines, fittings, nuts, bolts, screws and tools."*

PDS and Upgrades

Although the responsibilities for Post Design Services (PDS) and upgrades have never been clear, the stovepiping of IPTs and the DPA/DLO divide exacerbate the existing situation. When does PDS become an upgrade and is PDS exclusively a DLO responsibility? And at what stage or cost does an upgrade become a DPA duty, whether or not it comes under a partnering scheme between the DLO and industry?

With the drive towards clear MOD Customer–Supplier relationships, the answer to these questions becomes more important. Even if the answers become clear — and they haven't yet — the position is further muddied by the various stages of Incremental Acquisition projects. Responsibilities may hinge on where the risk lies and who is best placed to manage it.

Does anyone know the answer?

ORGANISATIONAL CHANGE – SUMMARY

Progress

- Empowerment of DCDS(EC) by placing Equipment Plan under his authority
- Empowerment of IPT leaders and DECs
- Improved performance within each IPT and DEC

Stagnation

- The DPA/DLO interface and and project/IPT transition causing hiatus at ISD
- Separation of procurement from support, and lack of Through-Life Concept
- Lack of resources and expertise of Service Customer
- Composition of high-level committees favouring Suppliers, not Customers

Regression

- Stovepiping of IPTs and DECs
- Role of senior managers in DPA, EC not adding value
- Loss of coherence in procurement output

Figure 1: Summary of Organisational Change.

CHAPTER THREE

PROCESS AND PROCEDURES

While so much effort was going into organisational change within MOD, it was perhaps inevitable that the more difficult task of streamlining procurement procedures was largely put to one side and buried beneath a surface mulch of hype and spin.

> *The task of streamlining procedures was buried by a surface mulch of hype and spin*

The objectives were good enough and, well implemented, would have contributed strongly to improved performance:

- The Downey Cycle to be replaced by the new CADMID Cycle with a reduced number of submissions to the Equipment Approvals Committee (EAC) during the development stages.

- Financial delegation to be increased.

- Funding for the first two stages of the new procurement cycle (Concept and Assessment) to be increased to about 15% of total development funding.

- Annuality to be a thing of the past.

- Incremental Acquisition to be the norm.

- A Through-Life Concept to be applied to all projects.

While the change at the first bullet above was largely cosmetic, and absurdly over-hyped, the other five would clearly contribute significantly to the 'faster, cheaper, better' elements of the Smart Procurement dictum. Increased financial delegation and the end of annuality would speed decision-making, while Incremental Acquisition would see equipment in the field much earlier; higher levels of early stage funding would provide a firmer base for a project, with a better final outcome; the Through-Life Concept would ensure that running costs would be minimised.

PROGRESS

The Procurement Cycle

The new CADMID Cycle has replaced the old Downey Cycle, and the reduction to two submission points (Initial Gate and Main Gate) has led to fewer returns to EAC. How much time has been saved by this is difficult to judge, as the third Downey submission which has been cut out was often a fairly quick affair. But it is fair to say that some saving in time has been made.

There are, however, a few concerns with the implementation of the CADMID Cycle. First, the shift of leadership from the Central Customer (EC) to the Supplier (DPA) is taking place too early. EC thinks capability, DPA thinks projects. Until the capability requirement is firmed up, we should not be looking at project solutions: by doing so, time can be lost, effort invalidated and unfortunate compromises set in concrete. The shift should be made at Initial Gate (although this may vary from project to project), even if an embryo IPT has been set up during the Concept Phase. This was the original idea, but the MOD's Acquisition Handbook does not cover this at all.

Secondly, and probably as a consequence of the first point, Initial Gate appears to be getting later, and this puts the squeeze on the Assessment Phase. More time in Concept means less work in Assessment if the envisaged ISD is not to slip; less work in Assessment means more risk at Main Gate; more risk in the later stages *Less work in Assessment means more risk at Main Gate* means greater likelihood of cost increases, delay and performance reductions. Not what is wanted.

24

McKinsey's idea was that, if the risk had not been sufficiently reduced, projects would fail at Main Gate. This is fine in theory, but when sizeable amounts of public money have already been spent, failing a project at any point is unlikely to be an attractive proposition. And if we ever commit 15% of the total to the early stages, it will become even less attractive. The result of skimping during the Assessment Phase is likely to be either a fudge or repeated returns to EAC, neither of which is what we want. Therefore, risk must be sufficiently reduced before Main Gate, and to achieve this Assessment must be given sufficient funds and time.

Overall, then, the transition to the new CADMID Cycle has produced some marginal progress in the time spent on making Committee submissions, but this advantage will disappear unless action is taken to correct the early shift to DPA in the Concept Phase and the time squeeze on Assessment.

Financial Delegation

Financial delegation has been increased. This undoubtedly speeds things up, with many more submissions being signed off at lower levels without full-blown submissions. Whether the new limits are optimal is debatable, but they still seem to err towards the prevention of fraud/incompetence rather than the maximisation of efficiency and minimisation of cost.

STAGNATION

Early Project Funding

In 1968, Downey recommended[8] that 15% of the total development budget should be spent on the early stages of a project, and in 1987, the Jordan-Lee-Cawsey report[9] endorsed the same funding level.

---

[8] *Report of the Steering Group on Development Cost Estimating*, Ministry of Technology 1968

[9] *Learning from experience: A Report on the Arrangement for Managing Major Projects in the Procurement Executive*, MOD, 1987

However, in 1988 the House of Commons Defence Committee[10] noted that only about 8% was being spent rather than the repeatedly recommended 15%. So, the Smart Procurement Initiative of higher funding of the early stages of a project is hardly new, but for over 30 years we have failed to achieve anything like the repeatedly recommended level.

While figures for the spend in the early stages of a project are notoriously difficult to determine, it seems that we are currently spending between 5 and 6% on Concept and Assessment. This buys you paper studies, but little more, and it is not until you achieve about 12% that you can do much more than paperwork. At the current figure, is it surprising if the necessary firm base is not established before approval at Main Gate sets tight cost, time and performance parameters, with consequent implications for managing projects within those parameters?

> *The necessary firm base is not established before Main Gate*

Of course it is difficult to increase funding for the early stages quickly because it is almost impossible to bring forward money in an overheated budget. But the sums are relatively small (10% of development spend) and should be possible to phase in over a period of time.

Incremental Acquisition

While Incremental Acquisition has, correctly, been lauded as a key component of Smart Procurement, there is little evidence of such an approach being applied. The MOD's definition remains unchanged:

> *"Incremental Acquisition provides for a capability to be upgraded in a planned way, from the initial delivery of a specified baseline capability to eventual achievement of a higher full capability."*[11]

---

[10]   House of Commons Defence Committee 1987/8, Fifth Report,
       The Procurement of Major Defence Equipment, HC 431

[11]   *The Acquisition Handbook*, MOD, Edition 4, January 2002, page 19

This definition is inadequate as it makes no mention of time. Who would want a 70% solution in a similar timescale to a 100% solution? Incremental Acquisition only makes sense if the 70% solution can be fielded within, say, half the time of the 100% non-incremental solution.

So, is it surprising that there is a paucity of examples of an Incremental Acquisition approach? One senior DPA man could only cite the Type 45 Destroyer as an example of a recent decision to go incremental – not a very good one. Yet, in the decades before Smart Procurement there were plenty. In the single land systems area that used to be LSOR 6, the following might well qualify under the title of Incremental Acquisition:

Rapier, Javelin, ADCIS, BATES, MLRS, AS90, HALO, Phoenix

In the case of ADCIS and Phoenix, the later incremental stages were subsequently cut (both ridiculous decisions), but this does not mean that the original strategy was not an incremental one. There are plenty more examples in other areas.

Yes, it is early days, but there does seem to be an unwillingness to follow such a path. Perhaps the last sentence on Incremental Acquisition in the Acquisition Handbook gives us a clue:

"Incremental Acquisition may also have disadvantages such as a lack of competitive pressure for later increments."

Is the fear of losing competitive pressure destroying the chance of making a major reduction in cost and time? It seems so.

But there are other obstacles to overcome with any future Incremental Acquisition project. Overlapping development stages means that it is difficult to determine the overall cost-effectiveness of the end result at Initial Gate and Main Gate, because development of the increments will not have started. This suggests risk, and risk is not attractive.

Yet risk overall is not likely to be increased by going incremental. Indeed the MOD Acquisition Handbook acknowledges this, for the

> *Risk overall is not likely to be increased by going incremental*

'Big Bang' approach imports as much risk as you can imagine, as we have seen with Land Digitization and BOWMAN over the last 20 years. Incremental Acquisition **reduces** risk by:

- Incorporating advanced technology only when it is mature.

- Reducing the complexity of the first all-important stage.

However, MOD procedures do not take account of this, particularly the Combined Operational Effectiveness and Investment Appraisal (COEIA) which is:

"A formal comparison, on a cost-effectiveness base, of particular equipment options (or combination of options) for satisfying an operational requirement... its purpose is to inform the decision to select one of the procurement options, and reject the others, before proceeding further with the project..." [12]

If the COEIA is to be carried out on a cost-effectiveness basis, and if that cost-effectiveness cannot be clearly established for the 'full' capability in an incremental project, the chances are that approval authorities will look more happily on other options where the cost-effectiveness can be established with more certainty.

Moreover, will the Central Customer (EC) wish to support an incremental approach if he is not confident that the first stage (say, the 70% solution) will be fielded in a much shorter timeframe? Probably not. So he will want a quantum leap in performance from a new system if it is going to take 20 years to arrive in service. And quantum leaps and long procurement cycles are still part of the underlying culture in MOD.

There are other concerns, too. Incremental Acquisition cannot work efficiently if the project is recompeted repeatedly, yet 'compete, recompete and recompete' is the DPA way.

Another concern has been expressed by Bruce George, Chairman of the House of Commons Defence Committee, who said[13] that his

---

[12] *Guidelines for the Conduct of COEIAs*, MOD DCS(SA), April 1996
[13] Bruce George, IIR Conference on Procurement, 24 September 2001

biggest concern is that Incremental Acquisition could camouflage the provision of worse equipment. This will certainly be so if the initial 70% solution does not come in much more quickly and/or if funds for the later increments are reduced, cut or moved to the right.

There are good excuses, then, for not pursuing Incremental Acquisition, but an effective incremental approach is vital if we are to reduce time and cost drastically, and to improve performance markedly. So, the excuses need to be rejected and this can only be done by strong political leadership and clear vision.

> *An effective incremental approach is vital if we are to reduce time and cost drastically*

That clear vision does not exist. Amongst those with a naval background (and we are going through a period when naval influence is very strong), there is a view that Incremental Acquisition is easy:

> *"Steel is cheap and air is free. So build large and keep plenty of space for whatever increments might be needed."*

But this is hardly the way forward for systems other than ships, particularly for land systems where size and weight are almost always very tight constraints, which makes it extremely difficult to allow for the output of the final incremental stage before the first stage platform design is agreed.

Others are not hopeful. An ex-MOD consultant with huge experience thinks that:

> *"Incremental Acquisition is a good idea if you can make it work, but it goes against the whole systems approach."*

It may be difficult, but it is not impossible if we tailor our bureaucracy to the required output rather than the other way round. But make it work we must.

The Through-Life Concept

While Incremental Acquisition is given one page of MOD's Acquisition Handbook, the Through-Life Concept is given four. MOD is taking it seriously. So, what has been achieved?

It is true that projects now have a Through-Life Management Plan (TLMP) from the start:

"To plan how to take a project through its life, across the CADMID cycle, meeting Customer needs and providing visibility to all stakeholders of the through-life management planning process."[14]

Very praiseworthy, but the general view is that they are badly done — perhaps not surprisingly for we all have to start somewhere. But the TLMP is about management procedures, not about reducing cost and time. And the problem here is that whole-life costing in the early stages of a project is hardly an accurate science, so that through-life aspects will inevitably take second place to procurement realities when EAC are being asked to endorse a selected option or options at Initial Gate or Main Gate.

It is estimated that 80% of running costs are locked in by the design before Main Gate, but if the running costs of the different options are not at all clear at that stage, then reducing or minimising them may be impossible.

> *80% of running costs are locked in by design before Main Gate*

But even if the running costs are clear, how often will decisions go in favour of the cheaper **whole-life** option, if that is the more expensive **procurement** option? The Equipment Plan is overheated, and procurement costs increases in the early years are most undesirable. It is not surprising that little progress has been made.

---

[14] *The Acquisition Handbook*, MOD, Edition 4, January 2002, p 11

Annuality

From the start, Ministers promised an end to annuality and its unsettling effect on the Equipment Plan, commitment to contract and project timescale. The previous Long Term Costings took a year and blighted the whole programme process by constructing anew the whole Equipment Plan once a year. At any given time in the annual process there was major uncertainty over what could be committed, what might be cancelled, what might be moved to the right and what might be changed in one way or another. All this was to go, and in its place would be a three-year cycle.

Whether anyone actually believed this is a mystery, but if they did, they were extraordinarily naive. You might perhaps expect this of new Ministers whose party had been out of power for 17 years, but there was no excuse for senior MOD officials. Of course, everyone wanted to believe it, and the line between the possible and the impossible was deliberately blurred.

For, whether or not the Government holds a triennial spending review, MOD has to work on an annual cycle to keep within that year's budget. The forecast of spend within the year keeps changing as projects and activities run early or late, increase in cost or are altered for a myriad of reasons. Yet, MOD still has to keep within the annual budget. These annual costings need to be as accurate as possible because overspending is a crime. Finding savings on an annual basis is no easier than in the past because the vast majority of spend in the early years is already committed — equipment projects under contract with penalty clauses, soldiers that have to be paid, or the running costs of ships at sea or aircraft in the sky. It is the last of these three that tends to carry the can if the spending climbs above budget, with ships tied up alongside, aircraft grounded and exercises cancelled. This is all highly visible to the media and damaging to politicians.

But, despite this, annuality is here to stay. The annual Equipment Plan man-oeuvres are very similar to the previous Long Term Costings, although the whole

Annuality is here to stay

31

process is now carried out by the staff of DCDS(EC), rather than by the old Programmes Staff who had dual responsibility to each single Service as well as MOD Centre — but not to the head of Operational Requirements who was nominally responsible for deciding what was needed.

For that reason we have taken a step forward, but annuality still plagues the whole process. And there is another problem.

Capability to Project

The transfer of leadership from EC to DPA, as already suggested, takes place too early. In other words, project solutions are being conceptualised and assessed before the capability requirement is clear. However, we are not only talking about the transition from one MOD organisation to another, but also about the filling of a capability gap by one or more projects. This sounds straightforward, but it is not. A capability gap is identified, ways of eliminating it (by land, sea or air) are assessed and the capability requirement is determined. However, the funding to meet this requirement still tends to be itemised as project lines within the Equipment Plan, because projects are easier to cost than capabilities.

Accurate costs are essential if the programme is to be clearly affordable. A multitude of wedges would hardly be acceptable, particularly if the length of the procurement cycle is reduced drastically thus ensuring that the transition from a wedge to a more accurately costed project takes place in the early years of the Equipment Plan when any increase is very difficult to accommodate.

There seems to be some confusion in the MOD's Acquisition Handbook which says:[15]

> *"The User Requirement Document (URD) identifies the capability that may, over time, be satisfied by one or several systems..."*

---

[15]   *The Acquisition Handbook*, MOD, Edition 4, January 2002, p 6

That is the theory, but it goes on to say:

"The URD consists of a complete set of individual user requirements..."

which now sounds as if it refers to a single project rather than the capability. This is confirmed by:

"... and maintains the user's requirement throughout the life of the system."

That refers very definitely to a single project rather than a capability or a combination of projects to meet that capability.

We have, therefore, a difficult change of gear which we have yet to master.

REGRESSION

The STP/EP Gap

DCDS(EC) constructs the Equipment Plan (EP) in detail ten years ahead, and less comprehensively for several years after that. However, the running costs of that equipment, including manpower costs, lie in the Short Term Plan (STP) under the responsibility of the Principal Finance Officer (PFO). While there may be friction at the interface between the EP and STP, this should be manageable.

But it isn't. The difficulty lies in the fact that the STP is constructed for four years only, as against the ten-plus years of the EP. Is it realistic to expect the construction of a reasonably accurate EP in years 5 to 10, when the detailed running costs have not been investigated? How do we know that we can afford the later stages of the EP? Does this not add more uncertainty to those that already exist in the process? If it does, should we not look at ways of eliminating this uncertainty? If it doesn't, why do we bother with years 5 to 10 of the EP?

Army chiefs fear that the EP is driving the size and shape of the Army, and that equipment decisions taken now (e.g. crew sizes, training equipment, availability levels, fuel consumption and a host

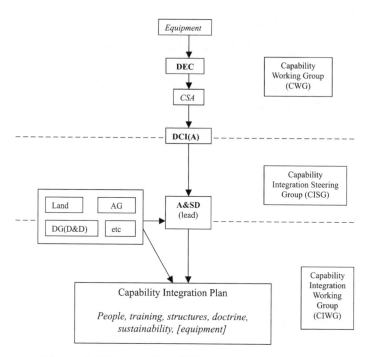

Figure 2: Director Capability Integration (Army).

of other parameters) will determine activity levels and the number of men and equipments that can be supported by the funds that will be available a decade hence. The concern is such that a new one-star post (Director Capability Integration (Army)) has been created to provide a bridge

> *Army chiefs fear that the Equipment Plan is driving the size and shape of the Army*

between the EP and the STP for the Army, as shown at Figure 2. Such a creation emphasises the seriousness with which the split between STP and EP is viewed by at least one Service.

The difference in duration between the STP and the EP is nothing new, but previously they were the responsibility of one part of the Ministry. Now they are in different areas. The split is exacerbated.

What has happened is that the difficult interfaces between the single Services have been replaced by a single difficult interface between equipment and the other lines of development (people, training, structures, doctrine and sustainability). There are MOD insiders who say that it is easier to manage the new interface than the old ones between the Services. That may be

> *A difficult interface between equipment and the other lines of development*

so, but only if considered purely in terms of constructing the STP and the EP as rows of numbers, but if output or outcome is the measurement, then we may find that it is not so. Indeed, the rows of numbers may well camouflage the gaps between STP and EP, which may not become apparent for many years to come.

Drowning in Process

Process has been elevated to the status of an ancient Greek oracle, at times somewhat Delphic, but at all times to be followed if disaster is to be avoided. The disaster is, of course, the career foul, rather than the tortures inflicted on mortals by the Greek gods. But just as terrible.

Although process has always been important, it was never quite so clearly etched in the text books as it is now. The Acquisition Handbook lays it down; follow it to the letter if you do not want to risk a mistake.

A well-defined process is important as guidance, but it should not be slavishly followed. However, many people have referred to the curse of 'rule by process' which stifles sensible decision-making, is a let-out for the incompetent and a cause of substantial delay when

> *The curse of rule by process is a let-out for the incompetent*

followed slavishly — as the less competent will always do.

"The tick in the box is alive and well."

"Process is more important than the project."

"We are all drowning in process."

"Process undermines project delivery. Is it all necessary?"

"It's all process – we have lost sight of what we are trying to do."

The above comments are from industry and various parts of the MOD, and are typical of the widespread concern that concentration on process is undermining effective decision-making. Of course process is important, but MOD seems to be concentrating overmuch only on parts of the whole process – the terminology, competition, placing contracts, the mechanics of getting to Initial Gate or Main Gate and all those 'activities' that are described in the Acquisition Handbook under the Acquisition Cycle.[16] This would be fine if all the other constituent parts of the Smart Procurement Initiative were also being carried forward enthusiastically, but they are not. As we have seen, such important components as Incremental Acquisition, the Through-Life Concept and partnering industry have yet to get off the ground and appear to have been placed in limbo.

Urgent Operational Requirements (UOR)

One of the most depressing developments is the increasing complication of the UOR procedure. Before the Falklands, the Gulf and the different Balkan operations, UORs were required to plug the gaps (sometimes serious, always important) caused by cuts or delays in essential equipment or upgrades. The system worked well with UORs being written and authorised within a week or less. But there was always a concern among the financiers that money could be wasted through this cutting of red tape and it was inevitable that there would be moves to plug this loophole, whatever the potential cost in lives.

> *A most depressing development is the increasing complication of the UOR procedure*

---

[16] *The Acquisition Handbook*, MOD, Edition 4, January 2002, pp 4–5

According to one MOD warrior, who has had extensive experience of submitting UORs before the Gulf, during the Balkan operations and for many years of the Northern Ireland troubles, this has now happened.

"UORs are now more, not less, complicated and require an extensive business case."

This may not matter too much during the present situation in Northern Ireland and elsewhere, but come another Falklands or Gulf or a new deployment against a capable enemy, this more complicated process could have very serious implications.

The emphasis should be on the 'urgent' in the term UOR, not on a complex process.

PROCESS AND PROCEDURES – SUMMARY

Progress

- Adoption of CADMID Cycle with fewer returns to EAC
- Greater financial delegation

Stagnation

- Levels of early project funding still way below recommended level of 15%
- Incremental Acquisition reduced from previous levels
- Through-Life Concept still a paper activity
- Annuality still a major source of turbulence
- Transition from capability to project

Regression

- Increasing gap between the Equipment Plan and the Short Term Plan
- Process is drowning delivery
- Increasing complexity of the UOR process

Figure 3: Summary of Progress in Process and Procedures.

CHAPTER FOUR

PARTNERING INDUSTRY

The Strategic Defence Review called for:

"A new relationship between the Ministry of Defence and its suppliers in which both sides can operate to their strengths, under formal partnering arrangements where appropriate, and which provides industry with the greatest incentive to perform." [17]

Stirring stuff. The relationship certainly needed a change, although there were (and still are) many people on each side who tended to look for change on the other side only.

PROGRESS

Relationships

There is little doubt that the relationship between the Ministry of Defence and industry has improved in general terms, with one senior industrialist referring to a 'sea-change' in their relationship with the Equipment Capability staff, where much effort is made to involve industry in 'rainbow' teams, small groups and briefings, although the one-to-one approach remains a key ingredient. In their relationships with the DPA, other industrialists have mentioned greater trust and transparency, more lateral thinking and a greater willingness to recognise the other side's constraints. One former DPA IPT member put it thus:

"Industry is working well with IPTs. There is greater trust, more recognition of DPA problems and a willingness to think creatively. Overall there is an improved combined approach."

---

[17] Strategic Defence Review (Cmnd 3999), *Supporting Essay Ten*, July 1998, p 10–3

And a DLO IPT leader said:

"There is a much clearer relationship with industry with greater trust and transparency."

This is encouraging, but these changes tend to apply to MOD/industry relationships in large, non-competitive projects. In competitive situations and with smaller projects (which form more than 90% of the total), the relationship is rather more cloudy with many MOD officials citing industrial attitudes of 'give us the contract and we'll do the work', while industrialists accuse MOD of old contractual 'them and us' and fundamental distrust.

Revealingly, a recent BAE Systems staff survey[18] showed up strong views that:

- Senior management was not making adequate changes to improve customer service.

- The company could not be relied upon to deliver on its promises.

Against that, many industrialists refer to a 'DPA culture problem' that sees innovation as a threat.

> *A DPA culture problem which sees innovation as a threat*

Partnering in Support

There has been a number of examples of partnering in the support of operational equipment where there have been gains for both MOD and industry. The partnering arrangement with Royal Ordnance is one example. The reduction in orders after the end of the Cold War led to overcapacity of ammunition production worldwide and undercapacity of production at Royal Ordnance, with the company being sucked into a downward spiral. To save the company, MOD looked for a mutually beneficial partnering solution. The start point was tested by competition and the price agreed represented a poor return to Royal Ordnance which was thereby forced to develop Gainshare initiatives. The successful outcome was, for MOD, security of supply and an even

---

[18] BAE Systems, *Response*, Issue 6, September 2001, pp 6–7

better price and, for the company, greater profit and insurance of future business.

Two other examples are worth mentioning here as good examples of mutually beneficial partnering: Challenger 2 and Pegasus engines for RAF Harriers.

The support of Challenger 2 is the responsibility of Vickers throughout the life of the tank and covers spares supply and base inspection and repair. The partnering arrangement between Vickers and the Army Base Repair Organisation (ABRO) is incentivised to reduce cost and improve turnaround times, and enables long term fleet management and optimisation of repair policy.

The Challenger Innovative Spares Provisioning (CRISP) programme is a seven-year contract to supply around 2400 consumable items, and is resulting in reduced holdings, zero obsolescence, higher availability and faster spares delivery to the unit.

The arrangement between MOD and Rolls Royce for updated Pegasus engines for RAF Harriers has been portrayed as a Win-Win contract after a 'spend-to-save' case was developed in partnership to overcome the lack of a programme funding line. As a result, MOD gained reduced lead time and a lower through-life cost, while Rolls Royce has achieved continuity of production and job stability.

There are other examples, particularly in warship support and PFI/PPP contracts. The latter, though, are difficult to evaluate as yet because the span of the partnering contracts and other contracts covers such a long period (15, 20, 25 or 30 years) and means that many of the advantages and disadvantages will not be evident for many years to come. Not only that, but it has been admitted that:[19]

"PPP is a failure because it has not been done well enough. PPP needs a more stringent customer relationship and there is not enough in-house expertise in private finance and contracting."

This will only delay any proper assessment of the value of PPP projects.

---

[19]   Kevin Tebbitt, *PPP in Defence*, RUSI, 26 June 2001

Partnering between the DLO and the prime contractor during the in-service support phase is relatively common as most large systems have a support prime contracted for many years – a prerequisite for successful partnering. But this was also the case prior to Smart Procurement (Rapier, for example) and it would be a bold man who would proclaim major progress in this area.

Modest progress, though, appears to have been achieved.

STAGNATION

MOD Attitudes

Some attitudes still remain entrenched in the old adversarial culture

While the Equipment Capability Customer and the DPA have, in general terms, improved their relationships with industry, attitudes in places still remain entrenched in the old adversarial culture. Most industrialists have pointed the finger at MOD contracts staff, but in reality there is a more widespread problem. As one MOD insider put it:

"When things go wrong, the old adversarial mentality returns."

One prime contractor executive thinks that:

"Defence procurement continues to concentrate too much on the financial 'value for money' aspects. Insufficient emphasis, if any, is given to many other factors."

The Bidding Process

Industry is often confused by what MOD says it requires because mandatory requirements, during the bid process or subsequent development, are downgraded to desirable or to 'less than mandatory'. While flexibility at the right time is laudable, it can be extremely provoking at others. This is particularly so when a mandatory requirement is downgraded in the middle of the competitive bid process to keep one or more competitors, who cannot meet such a requirement, in the competition; if one of his main advantages is removed, the effect on the remaining competitor can be devastating as he will have spent significant sums in developing a solution that will give him the competitive edge. As one industrialist put it:

"We no longer understand what is meant by the MOD term mandatory."

Linked with this issue of helping weaker competitors to remain in competition as long as possible, is that of trading-off cost, time and performance parameters which is the clear responsibility of the IPT Leader to remain within the 'box' agreed by EAC. However, as is the case most often, performance parameters are traded to reduce cost overrun or to reduce slippage. This leads to the perception that the User Requirement Document and System Requirement Document are 'set in jelly' and that work on meeting many of the specifications may well be wasted. The performance specification is a 'continually moving target' which, in a competitive context, can tilt the level playing field this way or that.

Competitive bids are now grossly overcomplex as MOD Invitations to Tender (ITT) appear to be increasingly detailed. One ITT in 2001, for a relatively simple equipment with little or no development, was five inches deep and the response ran to 6000 pages per copy and the total weight of the required number of copies was around one-and-a-half tons. Much of the complexity was brought about by the excruciating detail of the format required for the submitted bid.

This is not an extreme case, for a 2002 ITT (also for a project lacking technical complexity and development) was eight inches deep with similarly fine formatting detail.

Such unnecessary complexity increases the cost of bidding to anything up to £50M per competitor (depending on the complexity of the project or the ITT), and this does not include the cost of industry-funded work to develop a solution on which to base a bid. For a small project, the total bid cost to industry can actually exceed the likely profit for the winner. The result is that small firms get pushed out of the defence sector through collapse or migration to the Civil Sector, and larger firms recoup their costs from MOD at a later date on that project or another.

Partnering in Procurement

Formal partnering arrangements were seen as an integral part of the new relationship with industry. While some partnering arrangements have been struck in the support phase, particularly with Private Finance Initiative (PFI) or Public Private Partnership (PPP) deals, few, if any, exist in the equipment procurement phases. MOD spokesmen cite the Type 45 as coming closest to a partnering arrangement and there is no doubt that the MOD — industry relationship is working well in that project. Given that, it is surprising that partnering has not been embraced by the DPA.

Industry's view chimes with that of the original Smart Procurement Initiative:

"Unless we move to strategic alliances, we will be unable to deliver what we are asked to deliver."[20]

DPA's reluctance to embrace partnering in procurement is hard to understand, for it has struck some successful partnering deals in the support phase, notably in the maritime environment and with support for Challenger 2 tanks. The partnering arrangement with Royal Ordnance has already been mentioned.

Why can't this be translated into other equipment projects? The key factor is timescale. Gains from partnering will only become significant over time as examples show (Canberra over 50 years, Rapier over 25 years, many PPP projects over 20 or 30 years), and it is generally recognised that partnering needs a minimum of 7 to 10 years to become worthwhile. As this is much less than the average procurement cycle, there would seem to be no bar to procurement partnering.

> *Gains from partnering will only become significant over time*

But there is. It is called competition.

---

[20]   Andy Head, Raytheon, IIR Conference, 24 September 2001

Competition

No one thinks competition should be removed from the procurement process. Competition was retained under Smart Procurement as just one procurement tool among many, but its former position as the cornerstone of procurement policy has not really been eroded, and there is more than a whiff of 'competition for competition's sake'. As Sir Robert Walmsley put it:

> "The answer to the first question, is competition necessary, is that it remains my preferred method. It is not the only method. If I cannot have competition, I would rather have the ships and get them by some other way."[21]

This can easily be understood to mean that if competition is possible, have a competition, so it is hardly surprising if competition becomes *de rigueur* and selected rather more often than is sensible. And this is what is happening: 'competition for competition's sake'.

Good competition is worthwhile, but too often MOD has to prop up one or more competitors to maintain a semblance of effective competitive pressure. While claims from industry about MOD-managed leaks from one competitor to another are rare (and certainly not proven), the more insidious method of helping the weaker competitor(s) by downgrading mandatory requirements certainly does occur. And it takes effort and time — extra cost and extra delay. If an effective competition is not possible, then it makes no sense to hold an ineffective one. Competition is used too often. It is also used too frequently in one project. And it goes on for too long — at least until Main Gate, and sometimes beyond. This has four disadvantages:

- It is more expensive for MOD.
- It is more expensive for industry, which will in turn pass these extra costs back to MOD later in the project, or in another project.
- It drives many companies out of the defence sector.
- It makes partnering in procurement impossible.

---

[21] House of Commons Defence Committee Report on Procurement, 2001, p 5

The first two can be defended to some extent by the claim that competition drives down MOD costs by a greater amount than the cost of competition, so it is the third and fourth bullets above that are important.

Repeated and lengthy competition, much of which is only part-funded by MOD, is very expensive for the companies involved[22] with no guarantee of future work. This now makes many primes and sub-contractors hesitant about competing, thus reducing competitors and the possibility of effective competition in the future. Many will be put out of business or, where feasible, will migrate to the Civil Sector where profit margins are perhaps five times greater, timescales to production are perhaps a quarter, and innovation is sought after.

> *Repeated and lengthy competition is very expensive for the companies involved*

Even the largest companies are concerned over the cost of competition and the uncertainty which undermines investment plans. BAE Systems has been reported repeatedly as putting pressure on MOD to reduce competitive procurement and rely more on fixed price contracts for big programmes.

But the big issue is the effect that frequent and lengthy competition has on the viability of partnering in procurement. Partnering can only begin in earnest once competition has been concluded. MOD Guidelines for Industry states: [23]

"Consultation with the private sector on potential partnering opportunities should begin at the earliest possible stage of a project."

and:

---

[22] *Dancing with the Dinosaur*, Bill Kincaid, UK Defence Forum, December 1999, p 98

[23] MOD Guidelines for Industry, *Partnering between MOD and its Suppliers*, a joint note issued by MOD and CBI in September 1996

"Partnering arrangements will be a long (7 to 10 years) relationship since it is unlikely the full benefits of partnering can be realised in the short term."

In other words, start partnering early and finish competition early — exactly the opposite of what DPA is doing in most projects.

> *Finish competition early and start partnering early*

There is some trace of movement. DPA is occasionally dispensing with competition at prime level, provided that the prime carries out competition within the supply chain, although this risks disturbing any supply chain partnerships that already exist. Secondly, more development and production contracts are written to include several years of support after ISD. In theory, this provides the length of relationship required, but the hiatus at ISD, when the project leaves the DPA IPT and is passed to a DLO IPT, largely negates anything useful (such as Gainshare) emerging during procurement.

As a result, therefore, competition as currently applied by DPA effectively prohibits partnering during procurement in the great majority of cases.

Industrial Culture

There is still a widespread view in industry that Smart Procurement is something for MOD to do, and that when it has done it, industry can engage more effectively. There is little willingness to embrace change, just to watch it on the other side.

Sir Robert Walmsley, Chief of Defence Procurement, was recently very critical of the defence industry: [24]

"When did your car last go wrong, or your fridge or TV? So why does defence equipment go wrong?... I'd say I was on a mission to raise the game of the defence industry."

Some companies claim, perhaps not surprisingly, that they have changed considerably, although they will admit that they think

---

[24] Sir Robert Walmsley, *The Friday Interview*, The Times, 7 June 2002

the change is patchy. Certainly, attitudes at BAE Systems do not seem to have changed much at the top. The Carrier competition has seen them frequently criticise MOD for holding a competition and not giving the contract straight to the company. In a recent interview, Mike Turner, Chief Executive of BAE Systems, reiterated this view:[25]

"He wants BAE to be awarded most big prime contracts for weapon systems without competition. Not only that, he wants to be allowed to earn much more money from them."

And:

"BAE's argument is that it alone in the UK has the know-how to integrate complex modern weapons systems... he wants the MOD and BAE to be partners."

Is this arrogance? Or a plot to fleece MOD as so often happened in the cosy cost-plus era before 1985? Or frustration at the refusal of MOD to partner industry? There is, however, little indication here that the largest UK defence contractor has changed in response to Smart Procurement.

Nevertheless, industry has changed, but by how much and in what way is highly debatable. Ask any industrialist what changes his company has made to embrace Smart Procurement, and he is unlikely to give a coherent answer. Most changes cited are likely to be changes that industry has made in response to its own ability to win business, reduce costs and improve efficiency – changes that they would have had to make in the wake of the collapse of Communism, whether Smart Procurement had happened or not. Claims that the company is focusing more on delivery than on winning business have a hollow ring.

However, every company is different and each component part of a large company is different. This makes generalisations difficult. But, some changes do seem to have been made and these include:

- Focus on delivery rather than winning business.

- Reduction of sales empires.

---

[25]   *Plain Speaker Waves Union Jack,* Financial Times, 9 July 2002

- More lateral thinking.

- Reduced management layers.

But, the change is patchy and the pervading culture remains less than satisfactory as a dominant factor in shaping a smart partner for MOD. In particular, industry remains:

- Risk-averse.

- Short-term focused.

- Poor in marketing and management skills.

- Change resistant.

- Investment starved.

In addition, primes suppress innovation in the supply chain and are poor at controlling sub-contractors, while many Small and Medium-sized Enterprises (SMEs) are backward-looking, investment-starved and deficient in management techniques. Those SMEs in monopolistic situations are, by and large, not interested in change and are difficult to move out of their comfort zones.

Those in industry remain surprisingly ignorant about MOD as a whole. They know the DPA or DLO IPT with whom they interact, and some know the DECs, but few have any real idea about the other relevant organisations including the end user, the financial planners, the Joint organisations and the scientific scrutineers. Their whole strategy is not to upset the IPTs, XDs, DGs, CDL and CDP.

Industry, now, is not the smart partner for which MOD is looking.

Little progress here.

REGRESSION

SMEs

We have already seen that small and medium-sized enterprises (SMEs) find competition hugely costly, and that many are driven out of the defence sector. As primes are progressively squeezed by MOD, most SMEs find themselves squeezed more and more by primes who are increasingly interested only in low price and quick delivery from their suppliers rather than innovation. Indeed, innovation implies risk, and risk is wanted by neither MOD nor primes. SMEs fear lack of access to MOD, lack of knowledge, lack of business.

SMEs feel that they now have less access to MOD under Smart Procurement than previously and, therefore, less understanding of what is required. Most SMEs perceive that while primes flow down costs and risks, they do not flow down benefits, with the result that they have no motivation to 'buy in' to the project.

> *SMEs feel that they now have less access to MOD*

A comment extracted from the Defence Manufacturers Association (DMA) encapsulates a general feeling throughout the supply chain:

"The MOD's remoteness from its suppliers in future will benefit a few primes but disadvantage SMEs. Many small companies may lose interest in MOD business altogether."

No motivation, no SME buy-in. No SME buy-in, no technical innovation.

> *No SME buy-in, no technical innovation*

Although innovation can come from both primes and SMEs, technical innovation comes almost entirely from SMEs, not the primes. Yet the SMEs' ideas are channelled through the primes, who may have little interest in promoting them because their horizons are much nearer and consist of risk management, cost and time constraints – innovation can threaten all three. If the prime then suppresses the SME voice, will MOD even be aware of what it is missing? And even if it is, will it do anything about it? As one senior industrialist said:

"DPA sees innovation as a threat."

So SMEs are squeezed by primes and are more remote from MOD than in the past. The result?

"There will be an inevitable squeeze on supplier profit margins which is likely to provide the customer with short-term financial gain, but in the long-term could reduce options... the supply chain will be the weak link if the Government and MOD do not take their strategic responsibilities seriously".[26]

The disregard for, and the suppression of, innovation, the escalating and recurring costs of competition and the increasing remoteness of MOD are surely alarming for SMEs.

PARTNERING INDUSTRY – SUMMARY

Progress

- MOD/industry relations improved in some areas
- Increased partnering between DLO and industry in in-service support

Stagnation

- MOD/industry relations revert to adversarial under stress
- Bidding process too complex and costly; ITTs over-prescriptive
- Competition too frequent and prolonged in procurement phases
- Pervasive competition minimises opportunities for partnering in procurement phases
- No change in industrial culture

Regression

- MOD increasingly remote from SMEs
- SME technical innovation increasingly suppressed or ignored

---

Figure 4: Summary of Progress in Partnering Industry.

---

[26] *The Defence Aerospace Industry– the Supplier Perspective*, Nick Wilson, RUSI Journal, October 2000

CHAPTER FIVE

SMART PEOPLE FOR MOD

In June 1999, John Spellar, who then had Ministerial responsibility for Smart Procurement, summed up the importance of culture change in the MOD when he wrote:

"The [Smart Procurement Initiative] will not succeed unless we change the culture and our people respond to the circumstances we create for them... we need to become more flexible, responsive and receptive to new ideas. We need to depend less upon rulebooks or precedent and more on judgement and experience."[27]

And:

"We shouldn't be afraid to take risks, even if that means risking failure. If we fail, we should learn from our mistakes. Because if we never make mistakes we'll never change anything. My idea of the ideal public servant is not someone who never fails, but someone who always tries to make a difference."

Wise words. But not easy. No one would seriously expect such a fundamental change to take place quickly. John Spellar thought it might take more than five years; most people would expect it to take longer. But after more than three years, we should at least expect to see substantial progress.

After more than three years, we should expect to see substantial progress

---

[27] John Spellar, Under-Secretary of State for Defence, RUSI Journal, Volume 144, No 3, June 1999

A change of culture is not just a change in attitudes, for it is dependent on the underlying quality and expertise of the individual members of the whole body. It is imperative to make the best of every individual's ability and to eliminate their weaknesses by the right experience and training. And, then, to get rid of those who cannot measure up in the new environment.

How much progress have we made?

PROGRESS

Culture change

The vast majority of those in both MOD and industry would acknowledge that there has been a significant change in MOD culture, although they would qualify it as patchy and reversible.

The change is most marked in EC, where DECs are fully empowered and use that power, and in IPTs (DPA and DLO) where the IPT leaders are empowered and many, but not all, use that power to make decisions without referral.

The empowerment of DECs is the direct result of giving DCDS(EC) authority to match his responsibility (that is accountability) for the Equipment Programme. His predecessor (DCDS(Systems)) had responsibility, but no authority, the latter lying in the separate Programmes and Personnel area. DECs are responsible for their capability areas directly to DCDS(EC) and the Joint Capabilities Board. IPT leaders too no longer have a multi-linked management chain above them and are directly responsible to CDP. This flattened management structure may have some disadvantages (which were discussed in Chapter 2), but it does simplify and speed up the decision-making process. . . provided each IPT leader is strong enough to grasp his opportunity rather than hide behind procrastination. There are still

Some believe that the best way of preserving your skin is stick to old ways

54

those who believe that the best way to preserve your skin is to stick to old ways of doing business.

However, where empowerment is working well, individuals are more receptive to ideas from industry, they are better motivated and there is less bureaucracy. Day-to-day decisions are made more quickly, and the big decisions (at least at Category C and D levels where no committee submissions are required) are also made faster.

But in other areas, little progress has been made. Many people will point the finger at the DPA Contracts organisation as the area where culture change lags behind. Others are happy that the senior levels of management in the acquisition world have embraced the change of culture, but are worried that many at Grade 7 (Lt Col equivalent and below) have not. Senior officials in the DPA have referred to a layer of 'permafrost' where change is strongly resisted, and estimate that

> *A layer of permafrost where change is strongly resisted*

between 15% and 25% of their staff make up this layer. There are also many in Whitehall who are still suspicious of any culture change at all.

The culture change is real and considerable progress has been made, but that progress is under threat from those whose power is less than it has been and from those empowered individuals who shrink from the new accountability. And waiting in the wings are the Public Accounts Committee, the National Audit Office and the media who will be hard when mistakes are made by less-than-competent individuals or those without the necessary expertise or training. It will not take many costly errors for a call for greater oversight and less empowerment. Ministers and top officials will have to be robust in rebutting them, but they would be wise to have well-researched reasons to back up any general argument.

MOD Acquisition Training

Much effort has gone into improving training. Changes to existing courses, the addition of new courses and greater emphasis on training are all part of this improvement which is beginning to show at middle management level. The Acquisition Leadership Development Scheme (ALDS) appears to be filling a gap well, although there is some concern that there are not enough course places, itself a recommendation of its perceived worth.

However, acquisition training does appear to be DPA-centric, with other key acquisition areas getting less benefit. Whether this is because there is less pressure from the top in those areas, or whether there are fewer course places on offer is not clear, but if there is a problem it is hoped that the new Acquisition Training Cell, formed to coordinate the delivery of acquisition training across acquisition organisations, will speedily resolve it.

STAGNATION

Raising Personal Standards

With the exception of improved training, there is little evidence of rising personal standards in general, although motivation (through empowerment) has allowed personal performance to reach its full potential in many individuals. While there is some evidence that a few IPT leaders are more capable than the average project manager of the past, there is also a view that the average ability is much the same as before.

This is hardly surprising as most individuals within IPTs are the same individuals as previously. While some are better motivated, and others are better trained, many are neither, with the result that personal performance remains at a level rather lower than desired.

Some views from certain industrialists who work closely with MOD:

- It is proving difficult to move people out of their comfort zones.

- IPTs are full of old-style individuals focused on targets.

- There are plenty of dinosaurs still in existence.
- Too many deadweights not earning their salary, adding little value.

Or, to put it another way, in the words of another industrialist:

"Smart Procurement will only work if individuals are competent enough to deal with ambiguity."

Most are not; the talent is spread too thinly. Many question the ability of MOD management to conclude a genuine deal.

> *The talent is spread too thinly*

Motivation, Pay and Rewards

While empowerment may motivate DECs and IPT Leaders, the average long-term acquisition individual is not noticeably more empowered than previously. His pay is low in comparison with industry and he gets little or no reward if he does break out of his comfort zone. So why should he bother? If he is a capable individual, he will seek an IPT leader's post or leave to join industry; if he is less capable, he may well settle for a comfortable life.

Pay is governed by Whitehall scales, not those in industry, and there appears to be no flexibility in this area. Rewards, while unlikely ever to match those in industry, could provide some motivation at the lower levels, but little progress has been made in discussion with Whitehall. Currently, the agreed scale of rewards varies between 0.2% and 0.4% of salary with smaller (meal, flowers etc.) tokens for immediate recognition. This is a move in the right direction, but the immense effort that has been necessary to get this far suggests that the subject is not at the top of Ministers' concerns.

Of course it is difficult. Any increase in pay and rewards has to come out of the Defence Budget, which is severely overheated despite the extra cash provided under the 2002 Government spending review. However, there has been a huge increase in the use of specialist advisers or companies to evaluate bids and technical solutions during development to cover for the lack of expertise within IPTs. These specialist contractors are very highly paid in comparison.

Is there not an expensive imbalance here? If use of contractors is so essential, can we not reduce the number of DPA staff? And if we do that, can we not increase the pay of the remainder? Could we not then afford to recruit higher-grade staff and reduce the dependency on outside contractors? There's a magic circle here that we must break into. It should not be too difficult if a fairly wide perception is correct: that many IPTs are overstaffed and that movement between them to cater for peaks and troughs of workload does not happen.

Targets

Targets are inherently a good thing. They provide a clear aim point for those involved, and a benchmark against which progress can be measured.

But there are dangers. They are not easy to determine: set them too low and achievement will be too easy, thereby de-motivating the individuals or team; set them too high and 'failure' is certain. If 'failure' is synonymous with missed targets, it will generate a culture in which targets are set too low (to ensure 'success') and in which results are massaged for presentation to superiors and the public. In such a world, it is deemed better to achieve a 6% improvement

> *Badly set targets and fear of failure to meet them are counter-productive*

against a 5% target, than to make a 12% improvement against a 15% target. Badly set targets and fear of failure to meet them are counter-productive.

A good example is the Smart Procurement target set for (by?) the DPA: £2Bn over 10 years. At first sight, it seems a hefty sum, but it is only £200M per year within a budget of £5Bn – or just 4%. Hardly a revolution. Why was it set so low? To make sure it is achieved. Good publicity for DPA, MOD and Ministers. But bad for the tax-payer who should be getting a far higher saving from the huge amount of effort that has gone into Smart Procurement.

There are also 'Hard' (testing but achievable) and 'Stretch' (out of reach but not out of sight) targets within DPA, but these are not – and rightly so – publicised. However, there is an informed view that IPTs do not like these targets as they are designed to move them out of their comfort zones, so not surprisingly these targets are not as challenging as they should be. Comfort zones remain.

But the biggest disappointment of all is the adoption of targets set by the DPA and agreed with the Treasury, on cost and time. These are aimed solely at minimising cost and time overruns, not at significantly reducing the unacceptable length of the procurement cycle or the absurdly high cost of projects. Again, these are badly set targets that appear to be challenging but do not make any significant difference to the overall problem. After all, if the average project takes 20 years, will the elimination of three years of delay be significant? No.

The cost, performance, and time targets which are set at Main Gate have a mesmerising effect on many IPTs. They must be achieved – or at least seen to be achieved. Procurement cost increases and time delays are easily spotted by outsiders, so when they threaten to break out of the target 'box', something else has to give. And that something is performance, where reduction is often not immediately identifiable by those on the outside – whether it is a redefinition of the In-Service Date (ISD), a 5% decrease in mobility in certain types of terrain, a 3% cut in radar output power or a

> *Something else has to give, and that something is performance*

reduction in availability. Often the overall effect on battlefield performance of any change in sub-system or component performance is not clear even to the experts.

Once targets are set in concrete (e.g. at Main Gate), they can be a major constraint on innovative thinking. There is no sign of a more liberated attitude towards targets. Low targets to ensure achievement are still being set and used as a crutch to make decisions. Flexibility is being destroyed.

REGRESSION

Learning from Experience

Most large enterprises are not good at learning from experience, but MOD has perhaps been worse at it than many. Has this improved?

The first step — identifying the lessons — has perhaps improved, but there is still no way for IPTs and others to tap into these lessons easily. In a time-strapped world, sifting through acres of reports is not a realistic proposition. No real progress here.

The major change is the erosion of corporate memory. While some job tenures have lengthened, this is not a significant change overall, and the much greater movement between environments (a brigadier to run the Type 45 destroyer project, a ship's expert to run future artillery) means that professional backgrounds in each area have less depth. While the greater breadth has some advantages, the shallower experience is bound to reduce corporate memory where it is so often the detail, not the big issues, which become the show stoppers.

> *A major change is the erosion of corporate memory*

SMART PEOPLE FOR MOD

Progress

- Culture change in many upper and middle levels
- Empowerment of DCDS(EC), DECs and IPT Leaders
- Greater flexibility, better motivation, less bureaucracy
- Improved acquisition training

Stagnation

- Inherent personal standards remain limited
- Pay and rewards too low in comparison with industry
- Targets are too lax and too constraining

Regression

- Learning from experience undermined by loss of corporate memory

Figure 5: Summary of Progress on Smart People

CHAPTER SIX

RESEARCH AND TECHNOLOGY

The decision to decouple Research and Technology (R&T) from Smart Procurement remains inexplicable. It appears to have stemmed from a top policy move to privatise the Defence Evaluation and Research Agency (DERA), though the logic of doing that and not privatising other defence organisations (e.g. DPA) was never clearly expressed. It is tempting to blame the Treasury for seeing this as a money-spinner.

The reasons against privatisation were spelled out in *Dancing with the Dinosaur*[28] and these have not changed. But privatisation of DERA was not, and is not, the main issue. Far more important has been the repeated slashing of the R&T budget together with misuse of the remainder, while the DERA issue acted as a convenient smoke screen. R&T funding has no real supporters in either MOD or the defence industry — the short-termism that abounds in both places abhors spending money on an area where the return is measured in decades rather than years. But the defence industry is in a parlous state while many industries in the civil sector are doing very much better, and the reason for this difference lies in investment, including R&T. Do pharmaceutical companies and the oil industry sit on their hands waiting for government hand-outs?

> *Far more important has been the slashing of the R&T budget*

Investment in defence R&T is inadequate. Neither MOD nor industry invest enough, and this already inadequate investment continues to decline. Labour, before its election to power in 1997, pledged to reverse this decline:

---

[28] *Dancing with the Dinosaur*, Bill Kincaid, UK Defence Forum, December 1999, Chapter 7

"Decline in government sponsored R&D (by more than 17% between 1985 and 1994) has not been compensated for by an increase in civil research, which has decreased at an even faster rate... fears that the erosion of Britain's defence capability will become irreversible, and that the UK industry will become no more than an 'offset graveyard' with only a minor manufacturing role in 'off-the-shelf' orders placed abroad, have been voiced repeatedly."[29]

Far from reversing this decline, the Labour government has presided over an acceleration in that decline. DERA privatisation has effectively hidden the real problem.

PROGRESS

None

STAGNATION

None

REGRESSION

Process

One of the weaknesses in R&T has, for around 15 years, been the difficulty in pulling through government-funded technology into winning projects. Not surprisingly, this has led to hostility towards R&T on the part of all those who have responsibility for, or oversight of, budgets who see the R&T funding as so much wasted money.

A major barrier to pull-through has been MOD strategy which places the importance of a level playing field for competition later in the procurement cycle as more important than either making cost-effective use of R&T investment or producing world-class technology. As a result, joint MOD — industry research teams have not been

---

[29] *Strategy for a Secure Future*, Labour's Approach to the Defence Industry, October 1995

acceptable and this has made effective technology transfer impossible and, consequently, has ensured that such technology is not introduced into winning projects.

The position seems to have worsened. Technology transfer from the newly privatised QinetiQ would appear to have become more complicated, and pull-through to winning projects remains unlikely. No wonder the financiers call for less funding for R&T.

R&T Spend

Who cares about research? Not the public, not the Government, not MOD, not DPA, not even the Central Customer in the MOD who has the responsibility for applied research. With such little interest, is it surprising that the funds available for R&T continue to decline?

A Foresight report[30] states:

"Although the industry has in recent years been very successful in terms of delivering highly competitive equipment to both MOD and the export market, it is important to bear in mind that these successes are based on research and technology generation carried out mainly in the 1970s and early 1980s."

In those days, the spend on R&T was far higher. The report goes on to say that there is:

"... a widespread view that in defence and aerospace, we in the UK [are] rapidly consuming our technological inheritance."

> We in the UK are rapidly consuming our technological heritage

In the aftermath of the fall of Communism in Europe, the US reduced its defence budget but retained the same level of expenditure on R&T as before; in contrast, UK reduced its R&T investment by more than the fall in the defence budget. Now the proportional spend is:

10 (US): 4 (EU): 1 (UK)

---

[30] *National Defence Industry Technology Strategy,* Foresight Defence and Aerospace Panel, 2000

As a result, UK is being increasingly left behind in technology applications as the transatlantic gap widens. As R&T funding declines in this country, companies are increasingly transferring jobs to countries where the money is.

> *UK is being increasingly left behind in technology applications*

"It's no great secret that getting access to the US research and development spending budget is the only way to survive in the global defence industry."[31]

This is certainly what BAE Systems has done and now 40% of its jobs are in North America. This might be good for UK if technology transfer is possible, but most of the resulting technology will stay in US, and will translate into winning projects from US subsidiaries. No UK job creation scheme. The Department of Defense in US is now a bigger customer of BAE systems than is MOD.

And if not US, then elsewhere:

"Sir Richard Evans said that European governments were lagging behind the United States in supporting research and development in the aerospace sector. He gave warning that companies such as BAE Systems might consider transferring jobs to the Far East, where governments were prepared to make sizeable investments."

The cost of carrying out R&T in UK is comparatively high and this only accelerates the decline in comparison with other nations. This is very serious as UK is almost bottom of the league in the developed world, with government spending on R&D (not R&T) only 0.5% of GDP.

Nor do we spend the small R&T funds effectively. Most of the tiny government defence R&T budget goes on paper concept studies and

> *Nor do we spend the small R&T funds effectively*

---

[31] Sandy Morris, Analyst at ABN Amro, The Times, 31 January 2001

analytical investment studies. Only a quarter, perhaps, goes on technology generation.

There is a clear need to **increase** R&T spending on defence rather than to allow it to decline further. This is not impossible as the amounts are relatively small. The total MOD spend on technology generation is perhaps less than 1% of the defence budget, so a doubling of R&T funding would hardly upset defence long term plans. And this doubling could be further multiplied several times over without any new defence money.[32]

Of course, the defence industry must be coerced into investing more in R&T. That won't be easy because defence companies are happy to point out that the cost of bidding for competitive contracts is more than they invest in R&D and that, if competitions were fewer and less frequent, more money would be available for R&T. That is poppycock. Any savings would be channelled into other areas where the benefit would be seen at the next shareholder's meeting. Industry waits for R&T handouts as they rearrange the deckchairs on the stricken liner.

> *Industry waits for R&T handouts as they rearrange the deckchairs on the stricken liner*

And what is MOD doing? Reducing R&T spend and camouflaging it with such projects as Towers of Excellence and Defence Technology Centres which, while praiseworthy, are not likely to have any significant impact. These are desperate attempts to make the most of the reduced funding by channelling small sums of money into a few (six to start with) technology areas, while the remainder get sidelined. They are aimed at attracting investment from the private sector (good), but if this is achieved, will there not be a lobby to reduce government funding further? But even if that does not happen, these projects successfully draw attention away from the central problem — lack of R&T investment.

---

[32] *It's Only R&D But We Need It*, Bill Kincaid, Defence Review, Winter 1998, pp 49–51

"We need to be selective about the technologies we develop nationally or on a European basis, and be prepared to use US technologies in other areas in order to continue to make a leading contribution to multi-national operations."[33]

But, as the transatlantic technology gap continues to widen, the areas where US technology is not way ahead of Britain will quickly become fewer and eventually disappear. Then, 'buy US' will be the only cost-effective option.

Research Organisation

The privatisation of DERA did not go smoothly. The original plan to privatise the whole of DERA had to be amended to take account of US unease, and in the end it was only three-quarters of DERA which was privatised as QinetiQ, and the remaining quarter (consisting mainly of the higher-level analysis sections, and some specialist areas such as Chemical and Biological Defence) was retained under MOD control as the Defence Science and Technology Laboratory (Dstl). This arrangement seemed to answer the difficulty over the research relationship with US, and over the provision of impartial advice to MOD on investment decisions.

However, analysis depends on technical input data and that can only come from the privatised experts in QinetiQ. Is this a truly impartial system? Will the 'Chinese Walls' between QinetiQ elements hold when one element is providing impartial advice on competitive technical solutions while another is part of one competing team?

Of course, Dstl will ensure fair play and will channel the work to where it is best done – QinetiQ or elsewhere in industry. But does Dstl have the expertise and resources to do that, or will it just become a 'clearing house' for dispensing contracts? And how will it be able to assess progress adequately? All this is yet to become clear, but it does seem that the system and organisation is less robust and therefore less helpful to the MOD research customer(s).

---

[33] *Technology Towers of Excellence*, MOD, D/CSA/6/1/10, 14 July 1999

Technology Strategies

If research is to remain minimally funded and if we are to ensure that the maximum value is obtained from every pound spent, MOD and industry must coordinate their spending better to avoid duplication or funds wasted on fruitless research. This does not seem to be happening.

The problem of future competition has already been discussed, but there is also the problem of diverging technology strategies. The Foresight report[34] already referred to states:

"The study has shown that MOD and industry technology strategies are not completely in step."

And:

"Comparison of the content of the current version of the MOD Technology Strategy with that of the present document indicates that, while there are significant areas of common perception, there are also substantial differences in the ratings of importance accorded to various technologies. There also appear to be differing views regarding the need for support to ensure the continuation of certain defence-related capabilities."

This is due to be resolved. However, a combined strategy on priorities is not likely to be successful in overcoming the lack of R&T pull-through into winning projects unless it tackles the more difficult issues of MOD/industry R&T partnering and future competition.

Relationships

The formation of QinetiQ has undoubtedly changed the nature of the MOD relationships with industry and with other countries.

The US and, to a lesser extent, other countries are concerned about doing business in sensitive areas with a private company, whereas

---

[34] *National Defence Industry Technology Strategy*, Foresight Defence Aerospace and Systems Panel, 2000

previously they had no difficulty in dealing with the government-owned DERA. The retention of a quarter of DERA as Dstl was supposed to meet that difficulty, but will US be prepared to share research with QinetiQ in such sensitive areas as future tank armour? It seems doubtful. There is a decreasing number of research areas where UK is ahead of, or up with, the US with something worthwhile to offer, and this number will decline further and more quickly. The US will have less reason to share research with UK and, if it appears more difficult from a security angle, they will have little difficulty in shutting the door.

This may apply less to European cooperation, but this remains a rocky path and little progress appears to be materialising.

The research relationship between MOD and the UK defence industry could have been close while DERA remained in government hands, although the transition to an agency made DERA somewhat suspect in industry's eyes. But it was not this that made things difficult, it was DPA's insistence that joint research is inimical to a future competitive approach — that one possible future procurement competitor might gain an 'unfair' advantage by joining DERA in a research project. So short-sighted. The formation of QinetiQ would seem to have made a close relationship between MOD and industry even more difficult.

> *DPA's insistence that joint research is inimical to a competitive approach in the future*

The relationship between QinetiQ and MOD is distinctly different from that existing previously between MOD and DERA. The new relationship is less close and must therefore be characterized by tauter contracts, moving more towards fixed price. This means that:

- The Customer (EC with Dstl help) will need to be much more precise in stating his requirement. This is difficult to do in research programmes.

- The Customer must assess progress against milestones much more rigorously: to do so effectively, milestones may have to be restricted to rather meaningless ones on the lines of 'deliver a report'. Outcome will be difficult to build into clear research milestones.

- The Customer must write large numbers of contracts with QinetiQ and industry.

It is doubtful if ECC and Dstl have the expertise and resources to do all this.

The Future of QinetiQ

The objections originally raised[35] to the proposal to privatise DERA seem to be extant. Some of them have been fudged and others ignored, but none has been clearly answered. It is possible that privatisation will be good for QinetiQ, although there is still a significant possibility that it will not, for it may fail to win enough of the increasingly competed MOD research programme. This will not matter if it can rapidly increase its non-defence business, where profit margins tend to be much higher and pay-back much quicker.

Many industrialists have indicated their serious concern about the nature of their relations with QinetiQ in the future, few seeing them as likely to be easy or mutually beneficial. They

> *Many industrialists have concern about their relations with QinetiQ in the future*

also see a major opportunity to take business off QinetiQ as the research programme is increasingly competed. Will this happen? It will, if MOD allows it, for the major challenge for QinetiQ is the ability of its staff across the board. There are, of course, many highly competent and strongly motivated people but this is not sufficiently widespread. As is so often the case when individuals are paid or rewarded at a lower level than elsewhere (e.g. industry) the best leave

---

[35] *Dancing with the Dinosaur*, Bill Kincaid, UK Defence Forum, December 1999, pp 143–144

for where the grass may appear to be greener. And can QinetiQ reduce its charging rates to compete strongly with industry in most areas of research?

If it cannot win enough defence business, either MOD will need to nurse a lame duck, or QinetiQ must rapidly build up its non-defence business which will have decreasing relevance to MOD. In theory, MOD has a 'golden share' to ensure that it can steer QinetiQ in the direction that benefits MOD, not just QinetiQ. Unfortunately, this 'golden share' has no teeth. So, QinetiQ may fail or it may enjoy major success in non-defence areas. Either way, MOD will lose out and could be left with the Dstl rump and either a failed QinetiQ or one which is largely non-defence.

Such a major reduction in the defence research base will severely undermine our ability to tailor our forces in the immediate run-up to operations. As was discussed in Chapter Three, Urgent Operational Requirements (UOR) were extensively produced during the run-up to the Falklands, the Gulf and various Balkan operations. But even more important than the ability to write, process and have authorised these UORs was the ability of the then R&D Establishments and DERA to combine with industry to produce hardware in very short timescales — sometimes in a matter of days. This will be very much more difficult (perhaps impossible) if QinetiQ no longer has a wide base of deep defence expertise. It looks as if lives in the future are being placed at risk for savings which are so minimal that they cannot impact at all on the overall defence budget. This is irresponsible.

> *Lives in the future are being placed at risk for minimal savings*

RESEARCH & TECHNOLOGY

Progress

- None

Stagnation

- None

Regression

- Technology transfer and pull-through into winning projects more difficult
- MOD R&T spend still declining
- Proportion spent on technology generation declining
- Transatlantic technology gap widening quickly
- Formation of QinetiQ complicates relationship with MOD, industry and US
- QinetiQ may fail or become mainly non-defence, seriously reducing the research base
- Reduction of research base will reduce ability to tailor forces for operations

Figure 6: Summary of Progress on Research and Technology.

CHAPTER SEVEN

HOW MUCH PROGRESS SO FAR?

Whatever one's views about the implementation of Smart Procurement, there can be no doubt that some important progress has been made. This may be less than many would have hoped, but it is real and must not be left unsupported to become the prey of recidivists.

SMART PROCUREMENT: REAL PROGRESS

- Empowerment, especially of DECs and IPT Leaders
- Improved performance within each DEC and IPT
- Giving DCDS(EC) authority over the Equipment Plan
- Culture change in many upper and middle management levels
- DEC/IPTL relations and performance of Requirement Managers
- Low-level purchase card culture
- Greater financial delegation
- Small improvement in MOD/industry relations

Figure 7: Real Progress.

The single most important step forward has been the introduction of empowerment, particularly of DECs and IPT Leaders. This has improved motivation, speeded up the decision-making process and made individuals accountable for their actions. DCDS(EC) has also been empowered by being given authority over the Equipment Plan and over those who construct it, which was never the case with his forerunner, DCDS(Systems).

Empowerment has been a powerful factor in instigating a real culture change in MOD. While this culture change is only evident in some areas and is still

Empowerment has been a powerful factor in instigating a real culture change

a tender growth, it is thriving in areas where empowerment is both real and embraced – largely in the best IPTs and DEC areas. This culture change is marked by greater flexibility, more openness, less bureaucracy, increased motivation and more enthusiastic welcoming of new ideas.

At the lowest level, this culture change brought about by empowerment is illustrated by the success of the purchase card which significantly speeds up the buying process of small items. It is, as yet, too restricted in its use, particularly by the problem of which budget it supports or does not support. Progress, nevertheless.

The 100-mile separation of the procurement agency from its customer, and their supposedly tauter relationship might have been expected to distance the close association that existed between what was the Procurement Executive and Operational Requirements. This has not happened and, in general terms, the bond has been strengthened. True, there were close relationships before (e.g. artillery, ground-based air defence, armour), but they are now more numerous and more consistent across the board. Many links between DECs and IPT leaders are very strong indeed. Within this relationship, the IPT Requirement Manager is a key player. In effect, he has two masters, the IPT leader and the DEC, and he has to ensure that one is carrying out the design of the other. There was the potential for difficulty here, but it does not seem to have occurred.

Finally, greater financial delegation has resulted in speedier decision-making, particularly where small projects are concerned.

While real progress has been made, it is unlikely on its own to make the substantial improvements that the 'faster, cheaper, better' vision originally sought. It needs support. Unfortunately, many of the most important initiatives have hardly got off the ground.

> *Many of the most important initiatives have hardly got off the ground*

Culture change in MOD is patchy and reluctant, particularly at the lower levels. Senior directors in the DPA have referred to a layer of permafrost which resists any breakthrough and, although estimates of the thickness of this layer vary, this permafrost affects some 15% to 25% of the DPA, according to individuals within that organisation. Time may reduce this slowly, but only if pressure from the top is maintained.

SMART PROCUREMENT: UNHEALTHY STAGNATION

- Incremental Acquisition almost non-existent
- Through-Life Concept hamstrung by difficulties
- Culture change patchy and reluctant at lower levels
- Inadequate funding of early procurement stages
- Annuality remains a constant source of instability
- Competition remains too frequent, too prolonged and too costly
- Partnering with industry during procurement not happening
- Gainshare almost invisible
- Roles of EC CMs, DPA XDs and Support Directors not adding enough value
- Industrial cultures and attitudes largely unchanged
- Suppliers rather than Customers dominate MOD Committees
- Lack of expertise and resources of the Service Customer

Figure 8: Unhealthy Stagnation.

The importance of maintaining pressure is overriding for the culture change is, as yet, delicate. Even where the change is most marked, there is a tendency to revert to old-style adversarial ways when things go wrong.

Much effort has been put into culture change. Very little appears to have been devoted to other areas. There have been virtually no decisions in favour of Incremental Acquisition since the adoption of Smart Procurement, although there were plenty of examples in the 'bad old days'. Yet Incremental Acquisition is vital to the 'faster' element, and probably to the 'cheaper' and 'better' elements of Smart Procurement too. The bureaucratic barriers must be overcome, but there is no sign that they are being tackled.

The Through-Life Concept — crucial to the 'cheaper' and 'better' — is also beset by bureaucratic difficulties, which have apparently consigned this important initiative to the pending tray.

Similarly, funding of the early procurement stages — Concept and Assessment — remains at around 5% or 6%, rather than the oft-recommended level of 15%. This parsimony only increases risk at Main Gate, leading to a higher chance of significant delay, serious cost overrun and/or reduced performance.

Another issue is 'annuality' which was to have become a thing of the past, but which is very much alive and well. The annual Long Term Costings (LTC) round is dead; long live the annual Equipment Plan (EP) reconstruction. This annual reappraisal of the programme to ensure that its costs remain within approved and available funding, leads to annual cuts, delays or other changes, with consequent waste and programme uncertainty, some of which may later turn out to have been unnecessary or not in accordance with overall service or joint priorities. 'Annuality' is a Whitehall problem and cannot be tackled by MOD in isolation. Nevertheless, there seems to be no effort in train to tackle the issue. No movement here.

Partnering with industry was a major component of the Smart Procurement Initiative. Although there are several examples of part-nering in support phases, the commitment to frequent and prolonged competition in procurement has placed any realistic opportunities for partnering 'on hold', with little prospect of a green light in the foreseeable future. In any case, any reduction in frequency or length of competition may not change the light to green, because of the deep-seated suspicion of industry's motives and abilities that exists in MOD, and which is illustrated by Sir Robert Walmsley's depiction of them as "just big bureaucracies".[36] He may be right, but the tone of his remarks are hardly the tone of a man with a respected partner.

Industry has, in fact, hardly moved forward at all. Some will claim to have done so, but progress is slow at best and, in many cases, not obvious. Many defence companies think Smart Procurement is for MOD to do alone, and that when it has smartened up its act it will be a good partner for the defence industry, ignoring the fact that defence companies are:

---

[36] Sir Robert Walmsley, *The Friday Interview*, The Times, 7 June 2002

- Wedded to short-termism.

- Focused on winning business, not on delivery.

- Risk-averse.

- Lacking in good management techniques.

- Far behind many Civil Sector industries.

Some of this can be partially blamed on MOD's long timescales, uncertain programming and adversarial contracting, but much blame lies at the door of industrial managers. The potential rewards, such as gainshare, are going begging.

> *The potential rewards are going begging*

Within MOD, the required Customer/Supplier relationship is undermined by two things: MOD Suppliers rather than Customers dominate committees, while the Service Customer lacks the resources and expertise to carry out his acquisition responsibilities.

Finally, the management restructuring in MOD (EC, DPA, DLO) has resulted in flatter structure and shorter decision chains, but also in groups of experienced one- and two-stars without a central role. An important role for them has not been found, neither have they been axed. More of this in a moment.

SMART PROCUREMENT: ALARMING REGRESSION

- Increased stovepiping of capabilities and projects
- Increased stovepiping of MOD organisations
- Decreasing coherence of procurement output, including commonality
- Increasing divide between STP and EP
- Marginalisation of research and minimisation of technology generation
- MOD increasingly remote from SMEs
- Technical innovation in SMEs suppressed by primes
- Reduction of the future defence research base
- Reduction in ability to tailor equipment to operations at short notice
- Concentration on process is increasingly drowning delivery

Figure 9: Alarming Regression.

It should have been expected that a major new initiative might spawn some unexpected difficulties, and Smart Procurement has done just that. Whether or not those difficulties should have been foreseen is beside the point, but there should have been some resolve to tackle them as they appeared. This does not seem to have happened.

The most obvious drawback introduced is the stovepiping of capability areas and IPTs. As empowerment is embraced by DECs and IPT leaders, their domains, although more efficient and effective, have become more independent; greater independence means less coordination with parallel domains. Outsiders have mentioned that, while it is easier to do business with a particular DEC or IPT, it is much harder to do so if more than one capability or project group is involved. Stovepiping is increasingly a problem as capabilities and projects become ever more interdependent, and as digitisation and sensors become ever more central to every platform.

Greater stovepiping also applies to MOD organisations. Smart Procurement defines the basic relationship between the Central Customer (EC), DPA, DLO and the Second Customer (Cs-in-C) and makes each accountable for delivery within set targets. Inevitably this creates a stovepiping effect: IPT leaders focus on meeting their targets, not on future possibilities outside the immediate timeframe; DECs focus on closing capability gaps within the confines of an overheated equipment plan, not on running costs 20 years ahead.

All this decreases the coherence of procurement output: "I'll do my job, you stick to yours". As independence and empowerment are embraced, individual decisions are increasingly made without reference to others.

The decreasing coherence of procurement output

Competitive solutions are adopted lock, stock and barrel, with whatever components are bid. Commonality of components is reduced, a logistical nightmare is fabricated.

Despite the number of one- and two-stars without a central role, this lack of coherence is not being addressed. It may be tricky to regain coherence without undermining the benefits of empowerment, but consideration of this is not apparently on the agenda.

The divide between the STP and the EP appears to be widening. If equipment costs are planned up to 15 years ahead, but running costs are not, how can there be any real through-life approach? The Army is concerned enough to create a one-star post to try to bridge this gap, although there seems less obvious need for the other two Services to do so. The Army's approach has always been to equip the man, in contrast to the Navy and Air Force who man their equipment, and there is a very real possibility that the Equipment Plan is driving the future size and organisation of the Army. This may well be counter-productive.

MOD is becoming increasingly remote from SMEs, which are being progressively squeezed by primes with the result that technical innovation is suppressed.

As for research, the position is almost terminal. Decreasing funds lead to less technology generation which in turn reduces the chance that government R&T-funded technology will be pulled-through to winning projects; less technology generation means greater dependence on US technology and the export of jobs; the export of jobs undermines the UK defence industry. The future research base is likely to be severely reduced and this will, in turn, undermine our ability to tailor our forces for operations at short notice.

So how does the real progress achieved stack up against the stagnation and regression which exist?

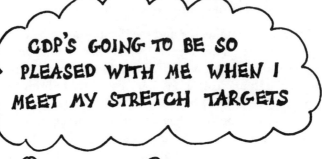

CHAPTER EIGHT

PROGRESS: GOOD, BAD OR INDIFFERENT?

The previous chapter pulls together those elements of the Smart Procurement Initiative where there has been definite progress, and those areas where not much has happened, together with problems which have emerged as a result of the changes made. But how can we evaluate overall change for the better?

The only sure way is to wait for 10 or 15 years, and then compare output (in terms of cost, time, performance) with the same output pre-1998. But, if we wait a decade or more before measuring our progress, we will only run the risk of pursuing wrong paths in a jungle of good intentions or drifting rudderless on a sea of indecision. We need to evaluate progress now. Inevitably such evaluation will be a subjective judgement, but if this subjective judgement is based on the honest opinions of enough people from a good cross section of those in the acquisition business, it should be pretty close to reality.

Marking Progress

Over the last nine months, I have interviewed and listened to the views of around one hundred different people in MOD and industry, at different management levels, and in different organisations. What is striking about their opinions is that almost without exception they agree with each other in essence, if not in degree. It seems a pretty solid basis for an evaluation.

But on what basis can we quantify qualitative opinion?

The Smart Procurement Initiative can be divided into those key initiatives which, if fully implemented, can together revolutionise defence acquisition, and those other initiatives which are enablers but which, by themselves, contribute little or nothing if the key initiatives are not implemented. Most organisational and many procedural changes are enablers, while those that by themselves markedly reduce time or cost are keys. For example, the adoption of the IPT concept is an important enabler, but without empowerment of the IPT Leader, will not reduce cost or time or improve performance to any great degree. However, the IPT concept will enable empowerment to make a major contribution towards the 'faster, cheaper, better' vision.

At Appendix One to this book, I have marked progress using the opinions of all those I have collected as a basis.[37] I have allotted more extreme marks (-10 to $+10$) for key areas (which are shown in bold) than for enablers (-2 to $+2$). Of course, this can be criticised — and has been — as inaccurate, but most of this criticism has been in defence of the critic's own area. The majority of those who have studied the markings believe it represents a reasonably fair view of the position today.

Significant achievements have been made by MOD in its reorganisation and internal relationships (including empowerment) where 41% of the changes required have been made. However, most of these changes have been the creation of enablers and

> *The greatest achievements have been made through MOD reorganisation and internal relationships, including empowerment*

therefore attract relatively low marks: reorganisation of OR into EC, PE into DPA, the single-Service logistics organisations into the DLO and formation of Capability Working Groups and IPTs. The key changes have been in empowerment of DCDS(EC), DECs and IPT leaders and in increased financial delegation. The major areas of stagnation concern the identity of Customer Two and his relationship

---

[37] This updates the marking I carried out in January 2002. The overall mark is almost exactly the same but there has been a shift between MOD reorganisation and MOD culture, in favour of the latter.

with DLO and ECC; the DPA/DLO interface and the transition of IPT or project from one to the other at ISD; and the consequential difficulty in initiating a true Through-Life Concept. And there is regression, too: stovepiping of IPTs and DECs, stovepiping of MOD organisations, the consequent loss of coherence in procurement output and the lack of clarity in the roles played by senior managers in EC and DPA.

Perhaps the best achievement is the change in MOD culture where again 41% of the change required has been made. The change of culture in EC and, to a lesser extent,

> *The change in culture is most marked in EC and, to a lesser extent, DPA and DLO*

DPA and DLO is most marked, with evidence of higher motivation, greater flexibility and less bureaucracy. Acquisition training has improved. However, the culture change is patchy and vulnerable to backsliding, and at lower levels there is a significant barrier of permafrost. While motivation has been stimulated in the middle management levels, pay and rewards are insufficient to motivate the lower levels who are continually dealing with higher paid and better rewarded staff in industry. Inherent personal standards remain limited and targets are too lax and too constraining. The most marked change for the worse is the dwindling corporate memory, as long-term tenures of specialist posts are phased out and more work is farmed out to individual consultants or consultancy companies, with the result that lessons are neither learned nor applied next time around.

Relations between MOD and industry have definitely improved, although the mark of 23% may prove to be a little generous. The most significant improve-

> *A lack of partnering between DPA and industry, primarily because of competition*

ments have been in trust and transparency, although this is very patchy and confined mostly to non-competitive large projects and tends to revert to the old adversarial ways when things get rough. Low-level purchase cards, too, are a good step forward, but their use is constrained by the inability to bill different budgets. What is clearly not happening is partnering between DPA and industry, primarily because of competition during the procurement stages, although some partnering is taking place in the support phases. The loss of any potential Gainshare is a major failure. Competition during procurement is too frequent and prolonged.

Industry has not embraced Smart Procurement and attracts a negative score (-14%), this regression being primarily due to the increased repression of technical innovation. MOD is partly to blame by making innovative bids too difficult, and by screwing down harsh fixed-price contracts with primes. Primes then pass these tough terms on through the supply chain, making innovation unattractive to either SME or prime. This is aggravated because MOD is becoming increasingly remote from SMEs. Without technical innovation, industry can hardly be a smart partner for MOD.

> *Industry has not embraced Smart Procurement*

New procedures and procurement techniques are, in overall terms, failing badly with a negative score (-5%). This reflects the lack of progress with Incremental Acquisition and the Through-Life Concept, the failure to fund early project phases adequately, the dominance of Suppliers (rather than Customers) on MOD committees, and the continuing uncertainty in commitment generated by annuality, together with the difficulties of progressing from capability requirements to projects. There is also serious regression caused by the growing gap between the 4-year Short-Term Plan and the $10+$-year Equipment Plan, the increasing complexity of the UOR process and an unhealthy fixation with 'process' which is drowning 'delivery'. Against this, the successful adoption of the (not very different) CADMID cycle, the reduction in EAC submissions and the trade-off decisions between time, cost and performance are small beer indeed.

Finally, the disaster that is Research and Technology. The regression (-97%) is almost total: funding, technology transfer, pull-through into winning projects, relations with industry and other countries, and general MOD attitudes towards research. In no area has there been progress. And what might be better

In no area of R&T has there been progress

for QinetiQ is not what is likely to be good for MOD or industry.

MARKING SMART PROCUREMENT	
MOD internal relationships and organisation	+41%
MOD culture change	+41%
Relations with industry	+23%
Streamlined procedures and acquisition techniques	−5%
Industrial performance	−14%
Research and Technology	−97%
TOTAL IMPROVEMENT	**+22% (excl. R&T)**

Figure 10: Marking Smart Procurement.

According to my marking, progress to date attracts a mark of 22% — that is, we are 22% of the way along the route to full implementation. This does not include the marks for R&T, which are so poor that it would unbalance the whole marking process.

Calibrating the Marking

As far as I am aware, no in-depth marking on a similar scale has been carried out either in industry or MOD, so there is nothing against which to calibrate my marking. Nevertheless, two senior MOD officials have given their views of progress.

At an IIR conference on procurement on 24 September 2001, the Chief of Defence Procurement listed areas where there was progress and where there was not. He listed the following as progress:

• IPT autonomy

• Customers with money (empowerment)

• Formation of the DLO

He listed areas where he saw little progress as:

- Whole-life approach

- Front-end investment

- Patchiness of the culture change

- Lack of gainsharing

This chimes well with my marking. As does the 'report card' presented by Air Vice Marshal Skinner and his panel to a logistics conference on 17 September 2001. He listed the following in the support phase:

- Whole-life approach – little progress

- Clearly identified MOD customers – no (this relates primarily to Customer 2)

- Trade-off benefits – yes

- Better relations with industry – no

- Sharper project delivery – possibly

- Sufficient early project investment – no

Again, this sits comfortably with my marking which was based on the views of 100 people from industry and MOD. And he went on to say:

> "Smart Acquisition in MOD has still to deliver in-depth improvements."

We are all saying the same thing.

Good or Bad?

My marking process was carried out in January 2002,[38] which was 33 months after the start of the implementation process. Is 22% after nearly three years good or bad? To many it will immediately look

---

[38] Although it was updated in July 2002, it is still largely based on input up to January 2002

poor, but it does suggest that full implementation, at this rate, would be achieved within a decade, a period that the less naive would have predicted at the start.

However, implementation so far has tackled the most straight-forward elements, including many organisational changes. That is not to say that these changes have been easy, but that what had to be done was clear and unambiguous. On the other hand many of the most difficult issues – such as partnering industry, Incremental Acquisition and the Through-Life Concept – are still at the starting gate awaiting riders. This suggests that the implementation rate will slow over the next few years and the full implementation period will be extended to 15 years... or 20... or more.

This likelihood of a decreasing rate of progress is born out by a similar progress marking I carried out in May 2000 after 13 months of implementation. Then I awarded a mark of 13%. So 22%

> *An improvement of 22% after 33 months does suggest a tailing-off*

after 33 months does indeed suggest a tailing-off. And what happens when progress on an initiative tails off? It is superseded by a new one. That could be a disaster – unless a new initiative has the same objective and takes account of progress made so far.

Will Smart Procurement Work?

But let us assume that in the not too distant future, implementation of Smart Procurement approaches the ultimate goal. Will that so transform defence equipment acquisition that we will be radically 'faster, cheaper, better'? No, it won't, for the simple reason that targets and expectations have been set far too low. So, while we may reduce ISD delays and limit cost overruns, we are only likely to reduce the average time from concept to ISD by about three years. As the average procurement cycle time is now about 20 years, reducing it to 17 years is hardly going to solve the major problems.

So, should we ditch Smart Procurement and look for some other alchemy? No, for significant progress has been made towards the objective and, by abandoning this, we shall have to start all over again. What we must do is protect that process, kick-start the many stalled elements of the Smart Procurement Initiative and seek ways of overcoming the difficulties that the changes to date have sparked.

And, above all, let us set ourselves real objectives and progress targets that will achieve 'faster, cheaper, better' to a degree that will allow us to cope with reduced defence budgets, shortening technology generations, changing doctrine and proliferating operational scenarios.

Smart Procurement will not get us there. What we need is an enhanced Smart Procurement Initiative. Let us call it Intelligent Acquisition.

> *Smart Procurement will not get us there. We need Intelligent Acquisition*

PART TWO

THE BONES OF INTELLIGENT ACQUISITION

CHAPTER NINE

THE CRUCIAL IMPORTANCE OF CYCLE TIME

Many of the elements of the Smart Procurement Initiative are aimed at reducing cost, but these are unlikely, on their own, to reduce cost by the amount that is both possible and essential. If we want to reduce procurement expenditure by some £2Bn to £3Bn[39] per year – around 20% to 30% of the combined DPA/DLO procurement budget – rather than the £2Bn over ten years that is the official target, we have to reduce time. As time is cost, a major reduction in cycle time should translate into a significant reduction in cost. As one executive in a defence prime contractor said:

"Nobody seems to realise that delay inevitably means cost as well. Delayed projects are more expensive projects."

Nobody seems to realise that delay inevitably means cost

And in a much reduced time-scale we can incorporate more mature technology, that is technology that has emerged from research and has been 'industrialised'; this will reduce technical, programme, schedule and cost risks without increasing obsolescence on fielding. Reduced risk tends to reduce time (and therefore cost) further, allowing firmer commitment to the programme. So, we have a magic Time Factor Circle, shown at Figure 11 which, once broken into, leads to increasingly shortened timescales and reduced costs.

---

[39]   *Dancing with the Dinosaur*, Bill Kincaid, UK Defence Forum, December 1999, pp 183–188

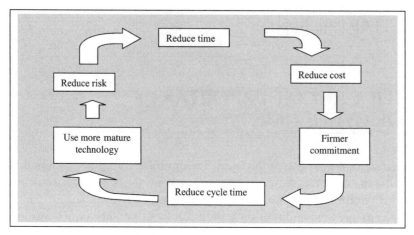

Figure 11: The Time Factor Circle.

Breaking into this circle is the problem. Where do you start? You cannot start by reducing cost, or by reducing the funds available for a programme, as the Treasury is hardly likely to look kindly on multiple loss-leaders or the users on much reduced performance. Nor can we begin by reducing risk, as this is not an independent parameter — indeed, neither are cost and time. One possibility would be Incremental Acquisition using maturer technology, but this will be of limited value if the full capability is still bound to a procurement cycle as lengthy as today's.

Reducing timescale by a large enough period (say, a 50% reduction), as a starter, is likely to do nothing but import risk and increase unscheduled delay.

That leaves us with firmer commitment. This may be difficult with the ever-present 'annuality' bogeyman, but surely possible. Once a programme is given the go-ahead, it should proceed to the next main decision point without hindrance or savings measures against follow-on stages, which only lead to extra studies of options, cost-reduction measures or delay to schedules. Firmer commitment and decision-making, in addition to reducing delay, will also shorten the originally envisaged procurement cycle.

Firmer commitment is what industry requires and it can also form the incentive for true partnering between MOD and industry. By committing more firmly, we break into the magic Time Factor Circle.

By how much can we reduce cycle time, once inside our magic circle? Mr Stephen Conver, formerly a senior official in the US Department of Defense and a Vice President of Lockheed Martin, has said:[40]

"There is no reason why you can't come down from a procurement cycle of 12 years to one of 3 to 5 years."

Our cycle is longer than 12 years, so it might be reasonable to expect a reduction from 20 years to 5-7 years. While this should become our longer-term goal, it might be sensible to set a shorter-term target of halving current cycle time (that is, to 10 years) within the next decade, with further reductions thereafter. And set a 'stretch target' of 7 years by 2010.

> *We should set a shorter-term target of halving the current cycle time*

Is this just fanciful? No. These sorts of cycle times are fairly normal in much of the Civil Sector, and in some areas overly long. The A340 aircraft was bought by airlines off the drawing board and was in service, on time, within budget in less than four years. This is no isolated example.[41]

So, it can be done. And, if we add a second key target of making, say, 90% of all projects incremental with the early introduction of the

---

[40] Mr Stephen Conver, RUSI Seminar on Smart Procurement, 29 January 1998
[41] *Dancing with the Dinosaur*, Bill Kincaid, UK Defence Forum, December 1999, p 183

70% solution (with guaranteed upgrade stages following on), the cycle could be shortened still further with Stage One entering service within, say, 5 years of the start of concept.

These figures are, of course, averages across the board. A large, complex platform with full development (e.g. a future Carrier) will take longer than an uncomplicated one where less development is required (e.g. a logistic vehicle), so we need to average it out when meeting targets.

If time is reduced by such a margin, costs will also fall substantially. Halving time will not halve costs, but it could reduce them by up to 30%. [42]

The high level of savings will allow some ISDs to be brought forward, but the early years will continue to be difficult, particularly if we increase the funding for Concept and Assessment to 15% of the total procurement budget, which is vital if we are to reduce risk early to contain later cost and time increases, and to make decision-making more straightforward. To overcome the early-years problem, we need to decide which programmes should be introduced earlier (primarily those which are essential to allow us to meet our new doctrinal requirement, and those which will reduce running costs by phasing out old equipment), and which should be started later to meet the currently envisaged ISD.

If cycle time is halved, there should be half the number of projects being managed in the DPA at any one time. So, DPA IPT staff could be halved. But rather than take this as a cost reduction, as so many would want, we should use most of the savings, if not all, to increase the pay of the remaining staff to keep the best and attract more capable entrants to the acquisition stream at all levels. These higher-grade individuals would make the whole process more efficient, more decisive, less risk-averse and more open to new ideas. This new dynamism would further cut cycle time and reduce costs.

---

[42] Ibid, p 184–185

Another advantage of much reduced cycle time is that there would be less disconnect between the output of applied research and full development. Today, by the time that the technology output from the applied research programme is required for incorporation after Main Gate (perhaps ten years later), that research has been overtaken by new technology and is wasted.

"There is a danger of serious mismatches opening up between the development times of major defence systems and those of their constituent technologies. There are examples of components and subsystems becoming obsolete – sometimes many times over – during the pre-production stages of the acquisition process ..."

and,

"All this points to the need for further acceleration of the defence business, learning from the reforms in the commercial sector, better understanding our dependencies on the world sources of technology and joint investment programmes." [43]

Removing this mismatch will reduce the risk of technology becoming obsolescent during development, with the inevitable consequence of delay and, as time is money, of cost increase.

Time is the key to revolutionising procurement. Unless we drastically reduce cycle time, we will not achieve the 'faster, cheaper, better' to the

Time is the key to revolutionising procurement

degree that we need to. We must concentrate, not on minimising delay and cost overrun as is the case today, but on halving the overall cycle time.

---

[43] *Systems Engineering for the Next Millennium,* Peter Brook, Journal of Defence Science, Volume 5, Number 1, January 2000, p 104

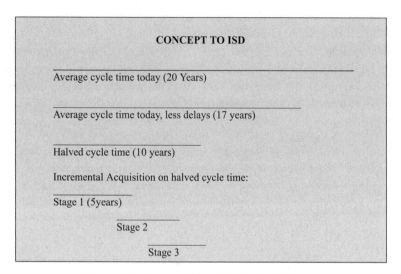

Figure 12: Concept to ISD Cycle Times.

And there are numerous examples to show how practical this is: UORs for the Falklands, the Gulf and the Balkans; the Joint Operational Command System (JOCS); the C-17 lease; and engineer tanks. There are many others.

If we now overlay Incremental Acquisition on halved cycle time, we really start to get somewhere, as shown in Figure 12.

The introduction of the 70% solution within five years (on average), and the 'full' capability within ten years, is what we should be aiming for. But is this really practical? Where can time be significantly reduced without importing major technical or programme risk?

From the start of Concept to ISD, we have an average time circle of 20 years, which needs to be shortened by 15 years if we are to meet this challenge. How?

> *We have a procurement cycle which needs to be shortened by 15 years*

Assuming that delays are largely eliminated, as CDP is confident of doing, we immediately find three years. What next?

The industrial work could perhaps be squeezed a little – but only a little – if there is firmer MOD commitment throughout. Firmer commitment means more continuity, smaller gaps between contracts, shorter start-up and restart-up times. But the time saved here will be relatively small – say, a couple of years from the pre-production phases of the procurement cycle.

We need to find another 10 years.

Before each of the main decision points – Initial Gate and Main Gate – it takes an age, on average, to write over-prescriptive ITTs, to submit bids, to evaluate those bids, to make submissions to EAC and to negotiate contracts, particularly if some of these activities fall at the wrong time of year when EP savings options are being considered. ITTs, in particular, are often ridiculously detailed, demanding a mountain of detail in response. One recent ITT was so demanding that the competitors were given a delay of a month on the date of the bid submission and subsequently MOD is taking four months extra over the evaluation (might this increase further?). Time lost to unnecessary detail. There is no reason why two years cannot be saved during these activities.

Next, we need to look to the Concept Phase which tends to drag on and on, as studies multiply and solutions proliferate. A good example of the time spent in and around Concept is the future infantry soldier programme which took 10 years from conceptualisation to Initial Gate. A comment in reply to the Defence Manufacturers Association survey in 2001 made the point in connection with another programme:

"Too much detail has been required by MOD in the Concept Phase. This has made assessment more time-consuming. The result is more delay and a likely change in the procurement strategy and the possibility of a re-bid."

Another factor is the gap between the end of applied research and the supporting operational analysis studies, and the official start of Concept. As a result, both the research and the operational analysis then need revisiting. Revisitation brings confusion if the new answers are substantially different from the original ones. Much time can be lost. Closer coordination between the research and Concept would reduce time in the Concept Phase. Reducing the detail required in that phase would speed things up further. A shorter period reduces the likelihood that major changes in technology or procurement thinking will have a serious impact. In any case, most Concept Phases start too early and the work expands to fit the time available.

Finally, we introduce Incremental Acquisition for most projects and bring in the 70% solution in half the time of the full solution.

So, cycle time can be reduced drastically

There, we have time reductions of:

- Three years through the elimination of delay post-Main Gate.

- Two years in the industrial work, given greater continuity by firmer MOD commitment.

- Two years through reducing complexities of ITTs and their evaluation, speeding up contract negotiations and EAC submissions.

- Three years by coordinating research and the Concept Phase, and starting Concept later.

- Five years by bringing in the 70% solution as Stage 1 of Incremental Acquisition programmes.

- Total: a saving of fifteen years.

If the A340 can be brought out in less than four years, there seems no reason why many, if not most, military systems can be fielded in a reduced capability form within five. Where there's a will, there's a way.

But do I hear a whisper from Sir Humphrey of: "Very courageous, Minister?"

CHAPTER TEN

INTELLIGENT ACQUISITION: MOD ORGANISATION AND PROCEDURES

The optimum MOD organisation and procedures are required to ensure that the faster cycle is supported as efficiently and effectively as possible. The Smart Procurement Initiative has identified most of the required changes, and many of these have been implemented, including the creation of EC as the Central Customer, the change to agency status at the DPA, the formation of the DLO, personal empowerment and the adoption of the new CADMID Cycle. In addition, other measures await effective implementation including Incremental Acquisition, the Through-Life Concept, and increased funding of early procurement stages.

The implemented changes are necessary and must stay, while those still at the starting gate must be kicked into life as soon as possible. But we must go further than that and overcome those problems, which have been either accentuated by the changes or have emerged as new issues. These include:

- The discontinuity at ISD when a project transfers from DPA to DLO.

- The incompatibility between the 4-year STP and the 10+-year EP.

- The upside-down committee world where Suppliers dominate the Customers.

- The stovepipe effect within EC and DPA.

- The unhealthy dominance of competition in procurement and ITT complexity.

Through-Life IPTs

The original concept of through-life IPTs envisaged a smooth transfer at around ISD from DPA to DLO:

> *"Through-life management of military capability necessitates transfer of management responsibilities for a project from the DPA to the DLO. Transition planning aims to provide continuous assurance to all stakeholders that the transfer of management responsibility will be achieved in a seamless manner."*[44]

This is, of course, essential. But is it working?

A project can transfer from DPA to DLO in one of two ways:

- Transition of the IPT from DPA to DLO.

- Transition of the project from its DPA IPT to a DLO IPT.

The first can only happen with a single-project IPT (e.g. Challenger 2, Type 45). As more than 90% of projects are managed in multi-project IPTs, only a small minority of projects can transfer with their through-life IPTs. The vast majority of projects are, therefore, passed from a DPA IPT to a DLO IPT. This obviously creates a major discontinuity with a change of IPT leader, a complete change of IPT personnel and a different managerial, financial and contractual climate.

But there is also a significant discontinuity when a single-project IPT transfers. In theory the IPT transfers complete, but in practice this does not happen as the DPA personnel remain at Abbey Wood and are replaced by DLO personnel at a DLO location. When the Challenger 2 IPT transferred, no personnel who had served longer than a few months in the DPA IPT transferred with it. In effect, the two methods of transition (bulleted above) are the same, with the project in both cases being 'thrown over the wall' at around ISD, and the DLO IPT often inheriting a support contract that they feel they need to change fundamentally. A severe discontinuity occurs; the through-life IPT is non-existent.

---

[44] *The Acquisition Handbook*, MOD, Edition 4, January 2000, p 28

Many people have suggested that the DLO and the DPA should be merged, thereby eliminating the interface that causes such a discontinuity. The opponents of such a merger point to the giant organisation that would be created and the difficulty of managing such a wide and diverse organisation. But to eliminate the interface that obstructs the through-life IPT, it would only be necessary to merge the DPA with part of the DLO – that part where the IPTs sit: Equipment Support and part of the Defence Communications Services Agency (DCSA). Then, a single IPT could steer a project through from Concept to Disposal in one location throughout, with a controlled change of personnel as the project reaches each new phase. Continuity, learning from specific experience and corporate memory would all be enhanced, while the damaging hiatus at ISD would be eliminated.

> *A single IPT could steer the project through from Concept to Disposal in one location throughout*

Committee Structure

One strange anomaly inherited and reinforced under Smart Procurement is the dominance of Suppliers over Customers on MOD committees in direct contrast to the theory that Suppliers are subservient to their Customers. Both CDP and CDL are members of EAC while DCDS(EC) and the Cs-in-C are not. It is true that the MOD customer is represented by VCDS, but he has a far wider remit than equipment and is not best placed to provide the necessary customer weight.

Similarly, the Master General of the Ordnance (MGO) is the equipment representative on the Executive Committee of the Army Board while his customer (Capability Manager (Manoeuvre) at two-star level) is not represented.

It seems nonsensical for the Suppliers on EAC, for example, to issue guidelines and targets to its own members to meet, and then assess their

> *If MOD Customers are to call the shots, they should be committee members*

own performance against these self-set targets. If the Customers truly call the shots, they should be the committee members, not the Suppliers who would more appropriately be 'in attendance when required'. It is, therefore, essential that membership of committees be changed as follows:

- DCDS(EC) and the Second Customer should replace CDP and CDL as members of EAC, with the latter two being 'in attendance' when required.

- The relevant two-star in EC should replace the DPA two-star on Service Boards.

The STP/EP Divide

We have traded the divide between the three Service budgets for a divide between operations and equipment. While there are those who say it is easier to manage than before, this is not a widely held view. According to one experienced Ministry budgeteer:

"Financial planning is a nightmare with no coordination between the STP and EP and no visibility of the STP by EP staff."

It is particularly difficult for the Army with its 22,850 platforms of 130 types, in comparison with the Navy's 43 ships of 5 types and the RAF's 451 aircraft of 13 types. The running costs of equipments tend to be several times the procurement costs, so the EP for Army equipments tends to have an inordinate effect on the STP.

There are two things that need to be done:

- Create a closer relationship between those who construct the STP and those who construct the EP.

- Place both on a common timebase.

The EP is the responsibility of DCDS(EC) and the STP of the Principal Finance Officer (PFO). If we try to place both under one man, we are likely to return to the position before Smart Procurement and throw away one of the principal steps forward — that of empowerment of DCDS(EC). This would be counterproductive.

So, reorganisation is out and that leaves closer working between the staffs of DCDS(EC) and PFO as essential.

This would be easier if both plans covered the same timebase rather than the very different periods which are covered now: 4 years for the STP and 10+ years for the EP. There is no obvious reason why the period covered by the STP could not be stretched to, say, 7 years.

Would a 7-year period be enough for the EP? If we succeed in halving the length of the procurement cycle, a 7-year period would cover the sort of ground that 14 years covers today, so it would be sufficient. There is no reason, of course, why EP planning needs to stop at the 7-year point, but detailed costings would only be needed for the first 7 years.

This common timebase would allow proper financial planning to be carried out, and equipment decisions would no longer carry the danger of determining the size and shape of the Army (and possibly the other two Services) in the future.

> *A common STP/EP timebase would allow proper financial planning to be carried out*

Stovepipe Effects

As a direct result of empowerment, performance within each capability area and IPT has improved, but coordination across more than one capability area or IPT has become much more difficult with the risk that future commonality of components may become nonexistent, while repair and resupply will be far more difficult. There has also been an increased stovepipe effect between MOD organisations (e.g. DPA and DLO).

The merger of DPA and the Equipment Support (ES) divisions of DLO (as recommended earlier) would eliminate the DPA and DLO stovepipe problems.

Similarly, there is an argument for merging the responsibilities of Customer One (DCDS(EC)) and Customer Two (the Cs-in-C), for the latter have neither expertise nor the staff to act as Customer Two, and many projects do not have one clear-cut C-in-C. Tanks, aircraft and ships, maybe, but not a lot else. Having one Customer for acquisition would clarify the current vagueness of the internal MOD Customer/Supplier relationship. There would then be one Customer and one Supplier for all procurement, spares and upgrades.

Stovepiping within capability areas and IPTs cannot be resolved by organisational means. The 'flatter' management adopted by EC, DPA and DLO is not really what it seems. The decision chains are flatter with DECs dealing directly with DCDS(EC) and DPA IPTs with CDP, but the previous higher management posts are still in existence and filled. It is these managers who could, and should, be given the clear task of coordinating output across DECs and IPTs. To do this they must have some executive authority and herein lies the difficulty: how do they wield this authority without compromising the empowerment that is one of the most significant areas of progress made to date?

None of the attempts to confront this problem to date appears to have been successful, and that may be because of organisation. For example, the two-star Capability Managers in EC are left in a supervisory role over what are largely (there are major exceptions) Service-oriented groups. Even if this was stirred further with the large Joint ladle, it would not change anything because EC, for all its Capability thinking, is still dominated by platforms. What is the EP if it is not a collection of funding lines for equipment projects, many of which are platforms, or platform dependent? The real issue is the capability given to platforms by C4ISTAR. But C4ISTAR cannot be split up into Service- or platform-oriented groups, and must remain a Joint and separate entity.

So how can we coordinate what goes on in the C4ISTAR DECs with what is being decided in the platform DECs? It is no use producing coordinating groups or liaison teams or suchlike. There must be someone (or some small group) with executive authority to override DECs in specific cases of stovepipe nonsense. At the moment this exists only in the Joint Capabilities Board, which is hardly the agile body needed to deal with day-to-day, detailed decisions. It is the CMs who need to be reorganised and reoriented to do this. How? This needs careful study, but some form of overlapping circles of authority may need to be established, linking CIS and ISTAR to the platform areas. Not easy.

In the DPA, the solution should be more straightforward. There are 6 two-star Executive Directors (XDs) and 10 one-star Support Directors (SDs) within the IPT structure. The obvious solution would be to make each SD responsible for the coordination between IPTs within his area, and give him the authority to overrule the IPT Leader, but only where he believes there is a clear coordination reason for doing so (e.g. to retain commonality in-service). This would happen rarely. More frequent would be the need for information flow on certain issues (e.g. BOWMAN, Land Digitization and FIST) between one IPT and others, or between a group of IPTs and industry.

This would be a real job for XDs and SDs, instead of the rather nebulous one given them to date and which are perceived by at least some of the IPTs as not adding much real value.

There are, therefore, plenty of senior managers who could bridge the gap between stovepipes, but who are only employed now on marginally useful activity. That they are not employed in core activity is due to a paranoia about resisting any

> *There are plenty of senior managers who could bridge the gap between stovepipes*

return to the 'bad old days' of Directors-General and Programme Directors, and adding length to the now admirably short decision chain.

This danger can best be avoided by giving XDs and SDs clear authority but equally clear limits to where they can use that authority.

Competition

Competition is the primary tool of procurement. It is applied whenever possible (often when not really needed), and it is retained for as long as possible, thereby making partnering with industry during procurement well-nigh impossible. Currently, it seems, there is a guideline (real or imagined) that competition is *de rigueur* and that there must be overriding reasons if competition is to be dispensed with.

Even if this is not the case, it is a comfort to many IPT Leaders, particularly those who are less confident in their ability to demonstrate cost-effectiveness without the crutch of competition.

As competition causes delay and is costly, at least in the early stages, for both MOD and industry, it should only be applied when there are good reasons for doing so:

> *Competition is costly and causes delay*

- When a strong competition is guaranteed.

and

- When NAPNOC and other contractual negotiation methods are unlikely to produce a clearly acceptable cost.

On no account should a competition be held when there is a clear leader or when there is a strong danger either that MOD will have to aid the weaker competitor(s) illicitly, which is unethical, or that the clear leader will perceive his advantage and inflate his price, which has happened more often than it should.

Competition reduces prices, so we believe. But so should partnering. If we reduce competition, we increase the possibility of mutually beneficial partnering and picking up rewards such as Gainshare, which should become substantial.

> *Reduce competition and increase mutually beneficial partnering*

But we can still have competition and partnering in a single project, although this is only possible if competition is completed much earlier in the cycle — say, by Initial Gate. If we get our act together on research, we could have the first stage of competition during research, with those that contribute the most to joint research teams winning through to compete in the Concept Phase.

The emphasis in competition in Concept would be on innovation, management ability and culture — not price. Once that competition is completed, MOD could then enter into a partnering agreement with the chosen prime and they could hammer away together at price and Gainshare.

Unnecessary competition is counterproductive. It must be limited in frequency and extent.

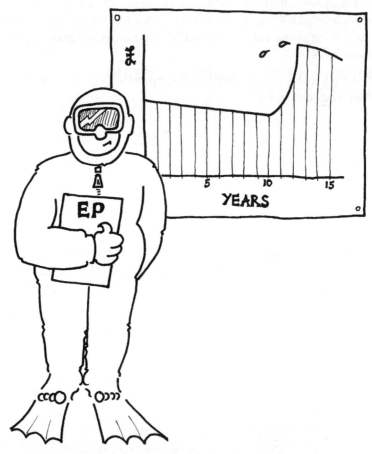

"HEALTH AND SAFETY DEMANDS THAT WE
DRESS APPROPRIATELY WHEN WORKING
BEYOND YEAR 10 ! "

CHAPTER ELEVEN

INTELLIGENT ACQUISITION: MOD CULTURE

Perhaps the most astonishing change brought about by Smart Procurement has been that in MOD culture. It is not yet spread as widely or as deeply within the acquisition community as it needs to be, and it is clearly reversible if pressure for change is removed, for the layer of 'permafrost' could well thicken if the procurement winter returns. Nevertheless, it has been warmly embraced in some areas, notably by DECs and IPT leaders. This progress needs to be protected, while efforts are continued to spread the change wider and deeper.

Culture change is perhaps the most difficult of all changes to bring about. Organisations can be reconstructed and processes can be reordered comparatively easily; indeed, most large organisations are continually changing both. But culture is much more difficult to alter, being deeply embedded in human beings. Changing how groups of human beings think, plan and work can only be brought about by clear guidelines on how their output must change and by giving them a clear perception of what is in it for them. Most humans are inherently selfish when it comes to career-building or job-holding, so they must be motivated in some way if they are to change.

Empowerment will motivate many of those to whom it applies, mainly at middle and higher management levels, and may well motivate the younger staff at low levels who perceive career opportunities. But it will not motivate those who have no new empowerment, those near the end of their career, and those at the lower levels with little hope of promotion. Nor will it motivate anyone who is more concerned about the downside of accountability rather than its opportunities.

Pay and rewards will motivate most. However, rewards need to be spread fairly evenly from top to bottom, but must be substantial. A maximum of, say, 0.2% of salary once or twice in a career is unlikely to motivate many to any significant degree.

Low-level rewards can still play a part in psychological motivation — making an individual feel proud of what he has contributed, making him feel a valuable part of a team — but psychological motivation also depends on making the whole operation seem worthwhile.

So what further measures need we take?

Leadership

The early days of Smart Procurement were marked by strong political leadership from George Robertson and John Spellar. It was this that generated the origin of culture change and then forced its early flowering. Since their departure, that political leadership has all but disappeared, and culture change has stalled in consequence. It is easier for recidivists to slide backwards without notice or correction; it is easier for the Dinosaurs to remain in existence.

Strong political leadership must be reintroduced if MOD culture change is to be carried forward. If it is not, the major progress that has been made will slowly wither.

> *Strong political leadership must be reintroduced if the culture change is to be carried forward*

Pay and Rewards

Rewards are all very well, but are not always easy to award fairly and they cannot be depended on by possible future recipients. If rewards are large enough, they will motivate, but if they are small, they will do so only marginally. Much more important than small rewards is higher pay.

The difficulty with increasing pay for EC, DPA or DLO civil servants and military officers is that it puts them out of line with their peers in Whitehall and the Services. However, acquisition staff are continually dealing with industry staff, whose pay is substantially higher, particularly in the civil sector. An MOD employee, who is struggling with children and a mortgage, may not weigh the advantages of pensions and job security fairly as he decides to take up an industrial opportunity. And it is the best who will go.

If the procurement cycle is halved, there will be a need for fewer IPTs and therefore fewer IPT staff. This would allow for a major increase in pay, either by boosting pay for each grade or by raising the grade of many jobs. The former would be simpler but would cause problems if acquisition

> *Fewer IPT staff would allow a major increase in pay*

staff were to be paid more than their peers elsewhere. The latter, however, would provide a clearer promotion path, the lack of which today is another block on motivation.

High-Level Decision-Making

In making equipment investment decisions, DCDS(EC) does not have a free hand. Major decisions on, say, changing the balance between ships and aircraft, or between aircraft and ground-based weapons, or even between manned and unmanned aircraft may well fall foul of individual members of the Defence Management Board (DMB) and cannot be made without their agreement.

Regrettably, the DMB is haunted by the spectre of inter-Service rivalry and the hand of history. While the EAC, despite its predominance of MOD suppliers, works reasonably well,

> *That means courageous decisions by the Defence Management Board*

the DCDS(EC)/DMB axis does not. This needs to be resolved by the DMB as a matter of priority. There is reportedly a £6Bn bow wave in the Equipment Plan and this can only be removed if courageous decisions are taken at the top — and that means courageous decisions by DMB.

If DCDS(EC) sat on both EAC and DMB, there might be some improvement, but the DMB culture must change. But here it appears to be Dinosaur country.

Innovation and Risk

Too high a level of risk, particularly in the later stages of the procurement cycle, tends towards delay and cost escalation; too low a level of risk suggests too much time wasted in the early procurement stages. Both play havoc with targets, and missing targets is not good for your health. So risk is eschewed. And, because innovation is tainted with risk, that is eschewed as well.

Innovation becomes a dirty word in a risk-averse organisation like MOD, and innovative ideas tend to be filtered out long before any decisions are made. Technical innovation from SMEs in the supply chain is suppressed by primes who demand cheaper components faster with penalties if not met, but in turn blame MOD contracts for not allowing them to exploit good ideas. Management innovation tends to do a little better as that is largely in the hands of the primes, but little of it appears in projects, which are governed by hidebound attitudes based on fixed processes. Only the best IPTs import management innovation.

Yet, innovative approaches are essential. The problem is that the risk attached to these is not understood by MOD. Exporting risk to industry, or even placing risk where it is best managed, only works if it is properly assessed. And it is only properly assessed by traditional methods if there is no innovation.

What we need is a more mature attitude to innovation, particularly technical innovation. We need to:

> *We need a more mature attitude to risk*

- Encourage innovative input during partnering.

- Award marks for innovation in competition.

- Remove the barriers to Innovative Bids.

The last is important. Currently, an Innovative Bid has to be separate from, and complementary to, the Compliant Bid; it must be to the same standard of detail as the Compliant Bid; and it must be fully costed. A competitor cannot submit an Innovative Bid without also submitting a Compliant Bid, but because the bidding process is so time-consuming and so costly, the additional Innovative Bid will not be submitted. I have seen this happen on numerous occasions.

To ensure that good innovative ideas are not lost in competition, the MOD rules for innovative Bids must be relaxed to allow a less detailed complementary bid to be submitted. In fact, the whole ITT/Bid process needs to be reduced from the monster it has become.

And if competition is reduced in frequency and length, innovative ideas will be much easier to put forward as part of the partnering process.

CHAPTER TWELVE

INTELLIGENT ACQUISITION: PARTNERING INDUSTRY

A new relationship with industry was a key component of the Smart Procurement Initiative, one which envisaged partnering between MOD and industry. In the words of the Strategic Defence Review:[45]

> *"A new relationship between the Ministry of Defence and its suppliers in which both sides can operate to their strengths, **under formal partnering arrangements where appropriate** ..."*

The let-out is the phrase 'where appropriate'. Nine months later, partnering had apparently been downgraded to 'team working' and the only reference to partnering dismissed as:

> *"The word 'partnering' will often be used to describe this new relationship with industry ..."*[46]

In contrast, there was much-increased emphasis on competition.

Partnering

What MOD has done effectively is to involve industry much more closely throughout the procurement cycle, providing more information than previously, seeking industry's views more often and asking them to share in the decision-making process through representation on Capability Working Groups (CWG) and IPTs. But all of this has

---

[45] Strategic Defence Review (Cmnd 3999), Supporting Essay Ten, July 1998, p 10–3

[46] *The Acquisition Handbook*, MOD, Edition 1, April 1999, p 23

been made much more difficult by the frequency and length of competition. Partnering, efficient team-working and involvement in CWGs and IPTs can only flourish once competition is complete and the final contractor selected. And the benefits can only start to appear once partnering and team-working are flourishing. This needs time.

Although the benefits of partnering and team-working are clear from what is happening in those few IPTs where competition is either not applied or has been completed, the vast majority of IPTs continue to apply competition as often, and for as long, as possible. This suggests to industry that the 'new relationship' is only the old relationship dressed up in fine words.

The new relationship needs a shot in the arm. If we are to adopt Intelligent Acquisition we need to:

> *The new relationship with industry needs a shot in the arm*

- Limit the frequency of competition.

- Conclude competition much earlier in the procurement cycle.

- Reduce the complexity and cost of the ITT/Bid process.

- Encourage innovation from SMEs in the supply chain.

- Find a way of incentivising industry to inject ideas into CWGs.

- Improve industry participation in IPTs in general.

Competition

As has already been discussed in Chapter Ten, competition must be used less frequently and must be completed earlier in the procurement cycle. This means amending today's policy on competition. Now, competition is chosen unless

> *Competition must be less frequent and completed earlier in the procurement cycle*

there are clear reasons for avoiding it; we need instead to hold competition only where the gains are obvious. In addition, competition should be completed by Initial Gate unless there are clear reasons for prolonging it.

"The best way to calibrate whether our suppliers are delivering us good stuff is by fair competition against foreign suppliers."[47]

Competition, it seems from this, is an aid for evaluating the worth of competitive bids. This is not what competition should be used for: it should be used to reduce prices, improve solutions and generate new ideas. The last two are rarely attempted and even more rarely achieved. The fixation on price reduction and the warm feeling generated by competition are the real reasons that IPTs hold competitions. As a result, competition has become an analgesic for the lazy and, like so many palliative measures, is so overused that it creates a dependency.

This dependency must be kicked. Competition must:

- Be chosen only where there is a clear gain to be had.

- Be selected only where a strong competition is possible.

- Be concluded much earlier in the procurement cycle — by no later than Initial Gate unless there are very good reasons for retaining competition rather than seeking partnering.

The ITT/Bid Process

Competition is expensive for industry. A company must, therefore, be able to make a strong case to its Board that there is a reasonably good chance of winning. Each loss will:

- Either make the company less competitive.

- Or, persuade the company to reduce its activities in the UK defence arena.

---

[47] Sir Robert Walmsley, *The Friday Interview*, The Times, 7 June 2002

Either way, MOD is undermining the UK defence industry and will become increasingly dependent on foreign competition.

The cost of bidding is huge. Estimates for bidding vary from £2M (for a small programme) to £50M (for a large, complex platform). The cost of bidding can even top the likely profits, although this is rare. Bidding costs in industry are higher than R&T investment.

Bid costs can, and must, be reduced by one or more of the following:

> *Bid costs can, and must, be reduced*

- Reduction of ITT complexity. Many ITTs are unbelievably detailed, not just on the technical specification and management plans, but on such things as format of the bid. Great detail is therefore necessary in the Bid.

- Reduction in detail required by Pre-Qualification Questionnaires (PQQ) or Requests for Information (RFI), especially when the company is well known to MOD.

- Speeding up the whole ITT/Bid/evaluation process, as keeping industrial teams together in the hope or expectation of winning is very costly. One recent ITT/Bid/evaluation/contract period will stretch to 18 months, even though the project is uncomplicated with little development.

Innovation and Innovative Bids

Innovation was discussed in Chapter Eleven. One manifestation of MOD's reluctance to champion innovation is the rules regarding submission of Innovative Bids, which are required to be to the same level of detail, and as fully costed, as the Compliant Bid. If the Compliant Bid is costly to prepare, the Innovative Bid is likely to be as costly. Doubling the cost is not a starter, so the Innovative Bid remains stillborn.

The rules need to be relaxed, although it is unlikely that MOD will do so during competition when there might be a perception from other competitors that the playing field has been tilted against them – and the DPA is very sensitive (oversensitive?) to that.

If competition is applied less often, then innovative ideas can be pursued more often by MOD with the selected prime and its sub-contractors and SMEs. And if competition is selected, but is completed by Initial Gate, innovative ideas (not Bids) can be discussed with MOD during competition and taken further once the winning contractor has been selected. If an innovative solution, rather than a compliant solution, is finally adopted, DPA should be robust in opposing losing contractors who whinge about unfair competition.

Industry and the CWG

CWGs exist in a variety of models, but there is a general perception that they do not engage industry effectively. The reasons for this include:

- Industry will not input its best ideas in the presence of future competitors. IPR is perceived as a problem.

- There are too many companies in any one capability area to involve in a working group.

- Selection of the most worthy companies only is held to upset the level playing field of future competition.

- Industry is best placed to input ideas on equipment solutions, not capability.

There is no real remedy, so it is probably sensible if industry is not expected to be included on a routine basis in CWGs. Instead, industry should be briefed regularly and meet one-to-one with DECs or their staffs, which is what happened in the best-run OR directorates in the past.

Industry and the DPA IPTs

Industry is a key part of a few single-project, non-competitive DPA IPTs, but it has proved much more difficult to involve industry during competition, and within multi-project IPTs where sheer numbers create a problem.

Again, there is no real remedy, but the reduction in, and earlier conclusion of, competition should help to some extent.

Industrial Culture

Industry needs to change its spots if it is to become a smart enough partner for MOD. Admittedly it is not helped by the patchy change of culture in MOD; by overbearing competition; by MOD's hostility to risk and innovation; by adversarial attitudes from many at the top and the bottom in the DPA; by MOD resistance to such important components of the Smart Acquisition Initiative as Incremental Acquisition and Gainshare; and by DPA's refusal to entertain partnering with industry seriously. Nor is it helped by the repeated demands of BAE Systems for MOD to ditch competition and give all contracts to them.

Smart Procurement is for both MOD and industry to do together. While MOD has made some very real progress, industry has not. This hardly encourages MOD to go further in its relations with industry. Industry must reciprocate. What does it need to do?

> *Smart Procurement is for both MOD and industry to do together*

Several key things are essential for progress:

- An industrial approach to partnering DPA and DLO in procurement, spearheaded perhaps by a much more innovative approach to Gainshare to persuade the MOD that there are major benefits to be had from partnering.

- A more enthusiastic approach to innovation, both in programme management and in technical solutions.

- Improved management expertise.

- Reduction of the myopia that exists in day-to-day decision-making, which tends towards crisis management as the norm.

Industrialists will point out that some of these are dependent on MOD making further progress. This may be so, but others are not. In any case, Smart Procurement depends on a coordinated approach by both sides. Where is industry's progress to date?

CHAPTER THIRTEEN

INTELLIGENT ACQUISTION: RESEARCH AND TECHNOLOGY

Research and Technology was not a part of the Smart Procurement Initiative and has not become a part of Smart Acquisition. This is a mistake. The result has been a steep decline to a position where the future of the defence industry in this country is seriously undermined and the ability to respond quickly to specific threats immediately prior to operations is gravely eroded.

The part-privatisation of DERA has contributed to this, but it is not the root cause. It would, though, be helpful if we could put the clock back and reform DERA as the government-owned research agency, but this is clearly not a starter. Let us look at what needs to be done in the future, where MOD owns Dstl, and a privatised QinetiQ will become less dependent on MOD funding and might slide smoothly into the Civil Sector. Such a scenario is highly likely, whereas retaining today's status quo of MOD being QinetiQ's major customer is improbable. The other likely scenario is the disappearance of QinetiQ either by collapse or complete takeover by a major company.

If we are to reverse the decline in Research and Technology we need to:

- Bring Research and Technology into the acquisition process.

> *We need to bring Research and Technology into the acquisition process*

- Reverse the decline in research funding.

- Allocate a greater share of funding to technology generation.

- Close the gap between applied research and the Concept Phase.

- Achieve greater technology transfer to industry and pull-through into winning projects.

- Establish partnering between MOD and industry in research.

Research and the Acquisition Cycle

Research is a vital part of the acquisition cycle, yet it has never been part of Smart Procurement, nor of the new CADMID acquisition cycle. Why is not clear, but the most likely explanation is that the overriding Government policy from the start was privatisation of DERA, and this was never going to sit comfortably within an Initiative where partnering with industry was a key component. Privatisation of DERA generated much heat but little light and became a smokescreen obscuring the real research issues. No Smart Procurement illumination was allowed to probe this obscuration.

It is essential that Research and Technology is brought into the acquisition organisation, process and financial system. Only by doing so will its serious problems be tackled. The MOD-based scientists have shown themselves to be limp-wristed, and this lack of a research proponent must be made good.

But it is more than proponency. Research programmes must be more strongly linked to projects.

Research programmes must be more strongly linked to projects

The Pre-Concept Gap

Scarce research funding is inevitably spread too thinly across the wide range of research programmes, with the result that the minimum work can be done. What remains unfunded at the close of a research programme is what can be called 'industrialisation' of that research so that it is ready to be absorbed into the Concept Phase of a project. This industrialisation is the norm in US research, with the result that its output is generally more project-friendly than that in the UK.

This industrialisation costs money and can only be done by reducing the number of research programmes, by a significant increase in research funding, or by partnering industry – or by a combination of two or more of these.

The link between research and the CADMID cycle must be strengthened by joining the two together, so that the effect on research of any slip in Concept (and vice versa) is clear. If a research programme is heading for obsolescence because of a slip in Concept (and therefore ISD), then decisions on cutting, delaying or changing that research can be made with clarity.

Funding of Technology Generation

Funding for research must be increased several-fold. This may sound like a nonstarter, but it is not, provided it is done in a series of steps.

The real issue is not research funding, but provision of funds for technology – in other words, not paper studies and support for investment decisions, but the generation and demonstration of technology. The first step is to double MOD spending on technology generation. As this is less than 1% of the whole defence budget, it is nonsense to say it could not be found, although the increase might have to be delivered over, say, a period of five years.

The second step is to spend this increased research budget more effectively, by reducing the proportion spend on paper studies and investment decision evaluation and increasing that spent on technology generation — that is from 1:3 to 3:1.

These two steps would increase funds for technology generation by 3.5 times.

The third step is to seek partners in industry to match this spend with new funds to carry out complementary technology programmes, thus producing a seven-fold increase in MOD/industry spend on technology generation — all for an increase of less than 1% of the defence budget.

> *A seven-fold increase in the funds for technology generation — all for an extra 1% of the defence budget*

Partnering Industry

Partnering industry is the key. Although made more difficult by the part-privatisation of DERA, the bigger stumbling block has been the insistence of the DPA that such partnering tilts the level playing field of future competition and cannot be allowed. Of course there have been examples of joint research (FIST is a good example), but this has only been in cases where strong characters have resisted the DPA's gnashing of teeth, and there are many examples where promising joint research programmes have been burnt on this altar of competitive correctness.

Partnering could take the form of joint funding of a single programme with shared rights over the results; or separate funding of separate but complementary programmes with access of both sides to all results; or joint MOD/industry research teams carrying out research together. It does not matter what form it takes — the key is that shared funding achieves the optimum output with full access to the results by all.

The formation of QinetiQ makes such partnering more difficult than it would have been with a government-owned DERA — but not impossible. At least, not impossible now. It will, however, become increasingly difficult in the future if QinetiQ progressively pulls out of many defence areas as would seem to be highly likely. What commercial company would remain in defence areas where future profits are small and return on investment is a decade or two away?

Still, partnering industry during research can be made to work and Dstl, as it strives to find its new role, must take the lead and take it quickly.

> *Partnering industry during research can be made to work*

Technology Transfer and Pull-through

An important consequence of joint MOD — industry research is that technology transfer from MOD to industry will be facilitated. Technology transfer is not effectively carried out by circulating papers and giving presentations; it can only be productive when made within the brain of a scientist or engineer, which suggests that industrial scientists working on MOD research programmes will effect technology transfer far more effectively. 'Industrialisation' of technology is also more likely to be achieved.

But it will all be to no avail if that technology is not pulled-through into winning projects. Even if the pre-Concept gap is closed, funding is increased, and technology transfer is efficiently made, that technology may not end up in winning projects often enough to justify the investment made.

There are many reasons for this, and include:

- The long procurement cycle, allowing newer technology to be incorporated later in the cycle.

- The prevalence of foreign technology, particularly US.

- The bias against innovation that exists in MOD.

The first and third of these have already been discussed, but the importance of each must not be underestimated. Both must be remedied.

The prevalence of US technology in most defence areas is more difficult to combat, and it is a problem that grows more serious every year. The MOD view is that it is only interested in value-for-money and if US technology provides it, then the tax-payer gets a good deal. However, it is not such a good deal if the defence industry, with its 350,000 jobs, is undermined.

It is time to recognise this and take a wider look at value for money for UK plc. MOD should select certain areas (not just a minimal six) where it wishes to remain an expert provider of technology in conjunction with industry. Within those areas opportunities should be identified, funding should be concentrated (the Towers of Excellence initiative could perhaps be adapted) and timescales scrutinised. Although there will be failures (inevitable in research), some excellent technology will be generated by joint research teams and this must then be pulled through into designated projects. Where necessary, this technology must be mandated in future competition.

> *Where necessary, technology must be mandated in future competition*

There will be many who will shy away from polluting the clear waters of pure competition, but as we have seen, purity of competition is destroying the UK defence industry, which is not a smart thing to do. The defence industry will depend for its survival on better or cheaper technology than that of its foreign competitors. Without it, it is dead. Or will be in ten years' time.

Not good for the UK economy.

Technology generation is vital. Let us tackle its problems before it is too late.

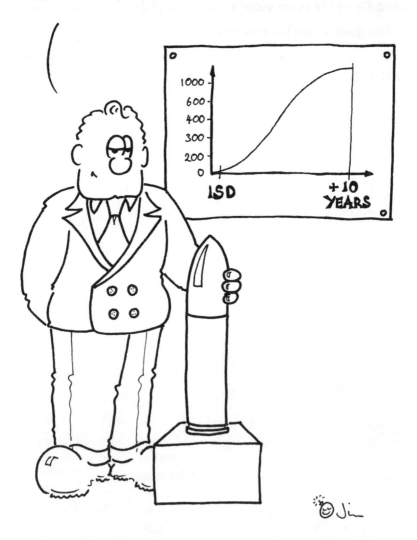

CHAPTER FOURTEEN

INTELLIGENT ACQUISITION: SETTING TARGETS

Targets are two-edged swords: set them too low and they are easily met, generating a false sense of achievement; set them too high and they will not be met which will attract blame and demotivate those at the working level. Too often, achievement of 6% improvement against a 5% target attracts praise all round, while an improvement on the same baseline of 12% against a 15% target will mean someone loses his job, or at least gains a black mark. Yet, the 12% improvement is twice as good as the 6% improvement.

Targets must be chosen with care. They should be:

- Challenging, but not clearly unachievable.

- Set by the Customer, not by those who have to achieve them.

- Clearly quantifiable objectives to be achieved by a certain date.

- Proof against 'fudging'.

Targets should also be divorced from the terms 'success' or 'failure' as it will never be possible to establish targets that are absolute measures of 'success'. What matters is whether the

> *Targets should be divorced from the terms `success' and `failure'*

group or team have sought to meet or better the target with energy, intelligence and initiative. Targets are but one tool in the overall assessment of performance and must be treated sensibly. If targets are set in concrete and missing them is 'failure', the energy of the team will be concentrated, not on doing their best to produce a good result, but on finding loopholes in the targets, on fudging the output and on spin in the presentation of that result. Redefining the criteria for ISDs is a favourite fudge, as is revisiting the input assumptions for down-stream support costs. There are many more.

MOD has failed in its target-setting for Smart Procurement. Many were set too low – for example, the overall saving of £2Bn within the DPA over ten years. It sounds a lot, but it is only some 4% of the DPA budget. 4% over 10 years? Revolutionary? I don't think so. Similarly, the targets set to reduce cost overrun and project delay – although quite difficult to achieve, successful achievement will make little difference to the overall average project cycle time of 20 years. In this case, the wrong targets have been chosen and have been set in isolation by a stovepiped organisation.

It is also rather meaningless to set targets as one single figure to be achieved over a period of time, such as £2Bn over 10 years, or 20% over 5 years. If the period is long enough, everyone will have moved on before proof of achievement or otherwise is available; forecasting success is easy.

So what targets need to be set? We need sensible targets on cost, time and performance on a year-by-year basis, and we need to add targets on manpower reduction as well.

Time

The key target is reduction of the average procurement cycle time. In Chapter Nine, I suggested that we need to start with a target of halving this cycle time (to 10 years) within a decade with a 'stretch' target of 7 years by 2010. This needs to be broken down into year-by-year targets which should show an accelerating reduction, as shown in Figure 13.

Procurement Costs

Significant reduction in overall cycle time will reduce cost and it has been calculated[48] that a 50% reduction in cycle time should be matched

---

48 Dancing with the Dinosaur, Bill Kincaid, UK Defence Forum, December 1999, pp 184-185

	2002	2003	2004	2005	2006	2007	2008	2009	2010	2011	2012	2017
Target	20	19.5	19	18.5	18	17	16	14.5	13	12	10	7
Stretch Target	20	19	18	17	15	13	11	9	7	7	7	7

Figure 13: Cycle Time Reduction Targets.

by a 30% cost reduction. We should therefore set our cost reduction target at 30% within a decade, with a 'stretch' target of 40% by 2010, the reduction to be made on both operating costs and equipment procurement costs, although not necessarily by the same proportion. Meeting the target would realise a total saving over 10

> *A 50% reduction in cycle time should be matched by a 30% cost reduction*

years of £6.7Bn, with an **annual** saving thereafter of £1.5Bn per year. If the stretch target was to be met, there would be a saving of £11.5Bn in the decade and an annual saving thereafter of £2Bn. Compare this with the agreed **total** 10-year saving figure £2Bn.

	2002	2003	2004	2005	2006	2007	2008	2009	2010	2011	2012
Target % Reduction	0	2	4	6	8	10	13	16	20	25	30
Annual Saving (£Bn)	0	0.1	0.2	0.3	0.4	0.5	0.65	0.8	1.0	1.25	1.5
Stretch Target % Reduction	0	2	6	10	15	20	25	33	40	40	40
Annual Saving (£Bn)	0	0.1	0.3	0.5	0.75	1.0	1.25	1.65	2.0	2.0	2.0

Figure 14: Cost Reduction Targets.

Of course, the Treasury would wish to take the whole of this large saving, but this should be resisted. At least some of the savings should be ploughed back in four ways:

- Reducing or eliminating the £6Bn equipment bow wave which distorts the whole programme.

- Increasing to 15% the amount spent in the early phases of a project.

- Bringing forward those ISDs which are badly needed, either for operational reasons or to reduce running costs.

- Increasing pay and rewards substantially.

Manpower

The cost reduction targets above would include savings from manpower reduction, which will be perfectly possible if project cycle time is reduced. If cycle time is halved, IPT manpower could be halved. Support groups could also be reduced, although this is likely to be by a smaller proportion. It should be possible to settle on a 30% reduction within a decade, with a stretch target of 30% within 7 years.

> *If cycle time is halved, IPT manpower could be halved*

	2002	2003	2004	2005	2006	2007	2008	2009	2010	2011	2012
Target % reduction	0	1.5	3	4.5	6.0	9	12	16	20	25	30
Stretch Target % reduction	0	2	6	10	15	20	25	30	30	30	30

Figure 15: Manpower Reduction Targets.

Cost Overrun and Project Delays

The current targets should be retained:

- Average in-year slippage < 0.3 month

- Average in year cost increase 0%

- Performance shortfall < 3%

However, these targets need to be clarified: what, for example, is a 3% performance shortfall? There is much scope here for creative figurework.

Performance

There is a real problem with setting equipment performance targets. If a radar, for example, only achieves 95% of the specified output power or discrimination, what is the performance shortfall overall? It could be negligible, or it could be very large. Of course, the targets can be tied to the meeting of project milestones, but translating performance shortfalls at those milestones is difficult. Usually, the MOD customer is asked to agree to accept a small shortfall in one or two parameters and, if he does, the performance milestone is 'passed'. The alternative is delay or fudging.

This is a real weakness in setting targets, for if performance targets are not clear and firm, they will be pillaged to meet cost and time targets. Not really what the User wants. The fudge in meeting performance parameters must be eliminated.

> *The fudge in meeting performance parameters must be eliminated*

CHAPTER FIFTEEN

THE PRICE OF FAILURE

Smart Procurement is a start. However, its implementation is patchy and there is major stagnation in many important areas, to say nothing of several significant problems which were not foreseen and which have been generated during implementation, and others which were never part of the Smart Procurement Initiative but should have been. Some of the stagnation and emergent problems may well be tackled successfully in the future, although it seems more likely that they will continue to be brushed under the carpet. But even if Smart Procurement is implemented to 100% of the official vision, the change will not be great enough to reduce time and cost by anything like the amount that is required to make a revolutionary difference. We don't want 4% reduction in costs, nor a 15% decrease in cycle time; we need to achieve what was unofficially the vision in the Winter of 1997/8:

"On time in half the time at 30% less cost."

As I have argued elsewhere, this is not wild fantasy but an attainable goal. If this is so, then we are wasting 30% of our equipment budget: £1.5Bn per year or, if we include the support phase as well, some £3Bn per year. £30Bn over ten years. More than another year's budget.

> We are wasting 30% of our equipment budget — £30Bn over ten years

That is the scale of our task.

Smart Procurement has not set out to achieve this scale of improvement and is, therefore, only a start. We need to do three things:

- Maintain the real progress achieved under Smart Procurement.
- Implement fully all aspects of the Smart Procurement Initiative, however difficult the decisions required may be.

- Adopt further measures to overcome the emergent problems and those not satisfactorily covered by Smart Procurement.

Let us call the combination of these three measures something different, such as Intelligent Acquisition, and apply it to the full acquisition cycle from research to disposal. The key measures as outlined in the previous six chapters are summarised in Figure 16.

KEYS TO INTELLIGENT ACQUISITION

- Cycle time is the key; halve it.
- Start projects much later and do them quicker; cut staff; pay the remainder much more.
- Maximise Incremental Acquisition, getting the 70% solution into service in half the time and guaranteeing later stages.
- Reduce competition significantly; complete remaining competition by Initial Gate, unless there are good reasons to recompete.
- Initiate partnering from Initial Gate; maximise Gainshare.
- Spend an average of 15% of development costs on Concept and Assessment Phases; allow adequate time for Assessment.
- Slash ITT complexity and overprescription; minimise bid costs.
- Reintroduce strong political leadership.
- Bring together STP and EP on to a common timebase (say seven years); find mechanism for linking DCDS(EC) and CsOS.
- Instigate courageous decisions on equipment at DMB.
- Replace suppliers (CDP, CDL, XDs) with customers (DCDS(EC) and CMs) on EAC and Service Boards; make DCDS(EC) a member of DMB.
- Merge DPA and DLO.
- Reduce effect of stovepiping through CMs, XDs and Support Directors.
- Develop a Defence Industrial Strategy to be owned jointly by the Treasury, DTI and MOD.
- Double MOD technology spend, encourage joint MOD/industry research teams, ignore effects on future competition and draw successful R&T into winning projects.
- Set stiff targets such as 'on time in half the time at 30% less cost' within 10 years and subdivide it into year-by-year targets, incorporating incremental and up-front funding targets.

Figure 16: Keys to Intelligent Acquisition.

If we do all these things effectively, we could:

- Save between £6Bn and £12Bn over the next decade.

- Save between £1.5Bn and £2Bn per year thereafter.

- Get the full capability into the field in half the time it takes today.

- Get the 70% initial capability into the field in a quarter of the time it takes today.

- Achieve a closer fit with technology generations.

- Ensure that equipment is not obsolescent before it enters service.

- Protect our investment in research by pulling-through technology into winning projects.

- Buttress the strength of the UK defence industry through joint research, partnering and a defence industrial strategy.

This combination of potential rewards should be more than enough to motivate ministers to redeploy strong political leadership, although the short-term nature of politics (the next Cabinet reshuffle, the next election, today's flavour) makes it unlikely that any politician will bother to press hard for an improvement that might make the lot of a future government of another Party that bit easier. Politics generates cynicism.

But what if we do not re-examine Smart Procurement or adopt Intelligent Acquisition? Or if we try and fail? What is the price of failure?

Cost

We will continue to waste between £1.5Bn and £3Bn per year. We will fail to resolve the £6Bn bow wave in the equipment programme with the result that programmes will be cancelled, moved to the right, or reduced in performance or numbers of units, tearing yet more holes in equipment capability. While defence remains so low in the list of voter concerns (even after September 11th), significant new money is highly unlikely to appear in the defence budget to close these capability holes, despite the outcome of this year's spending review. That extra money is likely to be spent on fighting terrorism; the bow wave is largely for warfighting.

Time

As I have already argued, time is cost. If we fail to reduce time by about half, we are unlikely to find large savings in the equipment budget.

And, if we fail to reduce time significantly, we will also remain in increasing conflict with the accelerating pace of technological change. In some cases technology generations are already shorter than the

> *In some cases, technology generations are already shorter than a single MOD decision cycle*

time it takes MOD to make one important equipment decision; this will become the norm rather than the exception, creating a tendency to lengthen the already lengthy decision-making process because technology will have moved on in the interim.

We will also find an increasing tendency for equipment to be obsolescent on arrival in the field. Someone else (the US invariably) will have fielded something better or cheaper or both during our deliberations. We will find ourselves with more TRIGATs. More waste, less capability.

Performance

The fixation on meeting targets, the empowerment of individuals to trade-off cost, time and performance parameters and the obsession with wall-to-wall competition is detrimental to eventual performance because cost and time targets and results are less easy to fudge. Cost and time parameters must, therefore, be met if 'success' is to be achieved. What is traded-off is performance, very often without a clear idea of what the battlefield degradation might be. This is likely to get worse.

Jobs

The UK defence industry employs around 360,000 people. It is big business. But it is shrinking. Six years or so ago, it provided 400,000 jobs and the rate of decline is likely to increase as companies invest more in the Civil Sector where profit margins are much bigger, timescales to production are much shorter and the marketplace is often easier to second-guess than MOD decisions. And it is the most efficient and the most innovative companies that are disappearing from the Defence Sector. Even if companies remain in defence, they are likely to follow investment to the US or create manufacturing jobs outside the First World.

The UK defence industry is under serious threat, but the Government has no defence industrial policy. Without an Intelligent Acquisition approach, the industry is likely to disappear except for a very few niche areas – the loss of, say, 300,000 jobs or more, although a proportion will be recreated in the Civil Sector. Without a strong indigenous defence industry we shall become more and more dependent on buying US equipment, often without the option of competition.

> *The UK defence industry is under serious threat and we have no defence industrial policy*

Operational Readiness

In the run-up to the Falklands War, the Gulf and the Balkans, many operational equipment weaknesses were overcome by dedicated work by the Research and Development Establishments (later DERA) and the defence industry working closely with MOD to meet Urgent Operational Requirements. This would not have been possible without a strong DERA and experienced companies, and more lives would have been lost.

The weakening of both the research organisation and the defence industry – and potentially the almost-complete loss of both – will make such action in the future virtually impossible. While we could buy much equipment from the US, we would find it impossible to modify our own equipment in a short timescale. And this will place servicemen's lives at greater risk.

> *Servicemen's lives will be placed at greater risk*

> **The Price of Failure**
>
> - Waste of between £1.5Bn and £2Bn per year.
> - Technology generations will become shorter than MOD decision cycles.
> - Obsolescent equipment will proliferate.
> - Performance parameters will be met less often or 'fudged'.
> - UK defence industry could largely disappear, with a loss of 300,000 jobs.
> - Operational readiness will be severely compromised.
> - More Servicemen will lose their lives.

Figure 17: The Price of Failure.

APPENDIX ONE: SMART ACQUISITION IMPLEMENTATION: THE ACHIEVEMENT SO FAR

MOD INTERNAL RELATIONSHIPS AND ORGANISATION				
Customer 1: the central MOD customer	Reorganisation from OR into EC	Complete. Capability-based. Empowerment of DECs creates stovepiping	Minor evolution	+1
	Formation of CWGs	Complete, but difficulties with including industry effectively	Minor evolution	+1
	Equipment Capability	**DCDS(EC) now accountable for the Equipment Plan**	**Revolution**	**+10**
Defence Procurement Agency (DPA)	Reorganisation into Agency	Complete	Minor evolution	+1
	Formation of IPTs	Complete, but empowerment of IPT leaders creates stovepiping	Minor evolution	+1
Defence Logistics Organisation (DLO)	Reorganisation into Joint Organisation	Complete, but little Joint culture	Minor evolution	+1
	Formation of IPTs	Complete	Evolution	+2
Customer 2: the frontline commands	Reorganisation to interface with Customer 1, DPA, DLO	Little observable progress overall. Resources allocated inadequate	No Observable Progress (NOP)	0
	Identity: Cs-in-C or COSs?	Not clear	NOP	0
Customer 1/ DPA interface	DEC/IPT interface	Working well. Requirements Managers (RM) effective	Evolution	+2
	CWG/IPT overlap	Extensive in some areas, particularly in the Concept Stage	NOP	0
Customer 1/ Customer 2 interface	Capability and equipment plan	Difficulties in meshing equipment with other lines of development. Army has created DCI(A) to resolve	Regression	−2

DPA/DLO interface	Transfer of IPT at ISD	No movement of staff with IPT; disruption at ISD	NOP	0
	Conveyor belt transfer of projects	Still 'thrown over the wall'	NOP	0
	Production & support contracts	Support contracts written by DPA still criticised by DLO	NOP	0
Customer 2/DLO	Interface	Vague	NOP	0
Empowerment	**Empowerment of DECs**	**DECs empowered**	**Revolution**	**+10**
	Empowerment of DPA IPTs	**IPT Leaders empowered. Some shortfall in commercial powers**	**Revolution in Progress**	**+5**
	Empowerment of DLO IPTs	**DLO IPTs empowered**	**Revolution**	**+10**
	Financial delegation	**Increased significantly, but strings attached**	**Evolution**	**+5**
MOD-wide relations	**Coherence of procurement output**	**Worse. Empowerment causes stovepiping between IPS and DECs, and between MOD organisations**	**Regression**	**−10**
ACQUISITION CYCLE AND PROCUREMENT TECHNIQUES				
Acquisition cycle	Adoption of new Acquisition Cycle	Complete	Evolution	+2
	Number of EAC approvals	Some reduction but less than envisaged	Minor evolution	+1
	Trade-off between cost, time and performance parameters	Happening, but often at expense of performance to meet time and cost targets	Minor evolution	+1
	Front end funding (15%)	**Small increase, but significantly less than necessary to minimise risk**	**NOP**	**0**
	Planning and profiling	Major interface problems between 4 year STP & 10+ year EP	Regression	−1
	Annuality	**Still disruptive, commitment to projects uncertain**	**NOP**	**0**

	PDS & Upgrades	DPA, DLO responsibilities vague	NOP	0
	Committee composition	Suppliers (CDP, CDL) on EAC and DMB), but customers (DCDS(EC), Cs-in-C) not	NOP	0
UORs	**UOR procedure**	**Increasingly complex**	**Regression**	**− 10**
Through life concept	**Adoption of Through-life Management Plan (TLMP)**	**Complete, but TLMPs poor**	**Evolution**	**+5**
	Procurement v. support costs	**Major difficulties in costing support years ahead.**	**NOP**	**0**
	Same prime for production and support	Allows continuity and partnering, but results in spares mark-up and lack of support expertise in prime	Regression	− 2
Incremental Acquisition (IA)	**Adoption of IA**	**Few examples of genuine IA projects. No sign of quick introduction of the 70% solution**	**NOP**	**0**
	Management of IA projects	Lack of clarity over DPA/DLO responsibility for later stages	NOP	0
RELATIONS WITH INDUSTRY				
Involvement of industry in MOD working groups	Industry in CWG	Difficulties with numbers of companies and IPR. One-on-one remains norm	NOP	0
	Industry in IPTs	Involvement post-Main Gate widespread. Less in competitive phases. Difficulties in multi-project IPTs	Minor evolution	+1
	Relations with SMEs	More distant	Regression	− 2
Acquisition methods	Contracting	Little change except in a few areas. Remains largely adversarial	NOP	0

		Bidding process	Too costly and complex	NOP	0
		Partnering in procurement	**Nil. Quasi-partnering in a very few cases**	NOP	0
		Partnering in support	**Many examples, but not much more than in past**	**Minor evolution**	**+5**
		Competition	Too rigid, too often, too late in cycle. Inhibits partnering	NOP	0
		Gainshare, sharing of disbenefits	**Very few examples, no significant examples**	NOP	0
		Trust and transparency	**Some real progress but less than required**	**Evolution**	**+5**
		PPP	Good PPP in support areas, but few examples in procurement.	Evolution	+2
		Purchase cards	**Working well at low levels, but use not wide enough**	**Evolution**	**+5**
		Defence Electronic Commerce System (DECS)	In development–too early to evaluate	Minor Evolution	+1
Joint training		Joint training in MOD	MOD courses more open to industrials	Minor evolution	+1
		Joint training in industry	Little change	NOP	0
SMART PEOPLE					
Culture		**Culture change in EC**	**Very significant**	**Revolution**	**+10**
		Culture change in DPA	**Patchy. Very marked in many IPTs. Some permafrost**	**Revolution in progress**	**+5**
		Culture change in DLO	**Patchy. Very marked in some IPTs. Poor elsewhere**	**Revolution in progress**	**+5**
		Culture change in Customer 2	Little as yet	NOP	0
		Culture change at top of MOD	**Marked in some places, but patchy**	**Revolution in progress**	**+5**

Personal standards	Raising personal standards	Some improvement in training courses, length of tenures and motivation, but Acquisition Stream lacks necessary teeth	Evolution	+5
	Pay & rewards	Small improvement, but still insufficient	Minor evolution	+2
Learning from experience	Identifying lessons	Immediate identification of lessons improved, but too subjective	Minor evolution	+1
	Communicating lessons	Still no way for IPTs to identify lessons from past. Corporate memory almost gone	Regression	−2
Targets	DPA targets	Declared targets far too lax. Hard and stretch targets not declared and are sometimes too lax	Minor evolution	+2
	DLO targets	Declared targets challenging, but delivery not on track	Minor evolution	+2
INDUSTRIAL PERFORMANCE				
Primes	Culture change	Little progress. Sees Smart Acquisition as task for MOD only	Minor evolution	+2
	Management	Still risk-averse with blame culture and short termism	NOP	0
	Innovation	Some non-technical innovation. Still tendency to wait for MOD to pronounce	Minor evolution	+2
SMEs	Innovation	Increasingly stifled by primes and MOD	Regression	−10
	Business techniques	Poor with insufficient investment. Poor knowledge of customer	NOP	0

TOTAL (excluding R&T) = **+80** (out of 372) = **22%**

151

RESEARCH AND TECHNOLOGY (Note 3)				
Funding	Applied research funding	Still declining rapidly	Regression	−10
	Technology generation funding	Proportion of applied research funding devoted to technology generation is far too low	Regression	−10
Relationships	Relations with industry	Worse with formation of QinetiQ	Regression	−10
	Relations with other countries	With US more complicated; with EU states unchanged	Regression	−10
Technology transfer	Technology transfer to industry and into projects	Increasingly blocked by IPR, competition downstream and formation of QinetiQ	Regression	−10
Process	Pre-feasibility gap	Gap between applied research and Concept still a problem. Little research TDP funding	NOP	0
Culture	Attitudes to research in MOD	Increasingly hostile	Regression	−10

NOTES:

1. Measures in **bold type** are those considered as essential to success and are marked as follows:**Minor Evolution +2; Evolution +5; REVOLUTION +10; Minor Regression − 5; Regression − 10**
2. Other measures are considered as enablers but will not, on their own, make Smart Acquisition a success. They are marked as follows: Minor Evolution +1; Evolution +2; Minor Retrogression − 1; Regression − 2
3. Research and Technology marks have not been included in the total as MOD (erroneously) does not see it as part of Smart Procurement. Additionally, inclusion would unbalance the whole marking scheme.

APPENDIX TWO: GLOSSARY

ADCIS	Air Defence Command and Information System
BATES	Battlefield Artillery Target Engagement System
C2	Command and Control
C4	Command, Control, Communications and Computing
CADMID	Concept, Assessment, Demonstration, Manufacture, In-service, Disposal
CDL	Chief of Defence Logistics
CDP	Chief of Defence Procurement
CIS	Command and Information System
CM	Capability Manager
COEIA	Cost and Operational Effectiveness Investment Appraisal
CRISP	Challenger Innovative Spares Provisioning
CWG	Capability Working Group
DCDS(EC)	Deputy Chief of the Defence Staff (Equipment Capability)
DCSA	Defence Communications Services Agency
DEC	Director of Equipment Capability
DERA	Defence Evaluation and Research Agency
DG	Director General
DLO	Defence Logistics Organisation
DMB	Defence Management Board
DPA	Defence Procurement Agency
Dstl	Defence Science and Technology Laboratory
EAC	Equipment Approvals Committee
EC	Equipment Capability
EP	Equipment Plan
IPT	Integrated Project Team
ISD	In-Service Date
ISTAR	Intelligence, Surveillance, Target Acquisition and Reconnaissance
ITT	Invitation To Tender
JCB	Joint Capabilities Board
LTC	Long Term Costings
MGO	Master General of the Ordnance
MOD	Ministry of Defence
MLRS	Multiple Launch Rocket System
NBC	Nuclear, Biological, Chemical
OR	Operational Requirements
PDS	Post Design Services
PFI	Private Finance Initiative
PFO	Principal Finance Officer
PPP	Public Private Partnership
R&D	Research and Development
R&T	Research and Technology

SD	Support Director
SME	Small and Medium-sized Enterprises
STP	Short Term Plan
TLMP	Through-Life Management Plan
UOR	Urgent Operational Requirement
URD	User Requirement Document
VCDS	Vice Chief of the Defence Staff
XD	Executive Director